SWISS
BERNESE OBERLAND

SWISS
BERNESE OBERLAND

A summer guide with specific trips
to the mountains, lakes and villages

Interlaken - Grindelwald - Wengen
Mürren - Kandersteg

Philip & Loretta Alspach

Intercon Publishing - Irvine, California

Note from the Editor

The writers have spent over 30 years visiting and
exploring the Bernese Oberland. The purpose of this
book is to provide helpful and useful information to
travelers about the area. The writers and publisher
have made every effort to include accurate and complete
information. They received no compensation or gratuities
from any person or organization to include information
in this book. The content and the selection of the
specific trips and excursions are the result of their
personal experiences and evaluation.

ACKNOWLEDGMENTS

We are grateful to the many people who contributed and helped us with this book. We thank each and every one, particularly Bruce and Maxine Alspach, Tom Beiseker, Bob Donovan, Liz Hallin, Suzette Jordan, Karen Murphy, Chet and Marty Rice, Buck Scott and Dennis Wilkinson. We offer our special thanks to Mary La Haye for editorial assistance and to Heidy Di Giovanni, Chalet Anita, Wengen, for advice and encouragement.

For invaluable assistance, we thank Eric Buhlmann of the Swiss National Tourist Office in Los Angeles.

Special mention to Walter Twerenbold and André Dähler of the Bernese Oberland Tourist Office in Interlaken; Hans Zurbuchen, Bahnen der Jungfrau Region; Markus Hügli, BLS in Bern; Walter Poffet, Grindelwald First; Alfred Seiler, Pfingstegg Bahn; Urs Schenk, Schilthorn Bahn; Jrène Schmocker, Interlaken Tourist Office; and the staff at the Grindelwald and Wengen Tourist Offices. And warm appreciation to Frau Beldi, Silberhorn Hotel, Wengen.

Thanks to the people at Digital Quickcolor, Inc., especially Ray and Diane Baggarley and Linda Barr for their creativity, flexibility and support. For computer assistance, our thanks to Bernie Nathan.

Sincere thanks to our friends and associates who offered invaluable input and significant encouragement.

MAPS

The maps were produced by Linda Barr with the exception of the map on page 17 provided by BLS Bern.

PHOTOGRAPHS

The photographs are reproduced with the kind permission of the Swiss National Tourist Office, the Bernese Oberland Tourist Office, the Jungfrau Bahn, First Bahn, Schilthorn Bahn and BLS Bahn. The writers contributed several of their photographs.

TABLE OF CONTENTS

PREFACE

Many travel books have been written about Switzerland. We believe this is the first book to cover the many facets of this area of the Bernese Oberland. This is "the most beautiful part of the world" with majestic mountains, clear lakes and green valleys. It describes the mountains, lakes, trains, funiculars, cableways, steamers, and the food and the wine. There are specific suggestions of things to do, trips to take, whether you have one, two or ten days to enjoy in the "playground of Europe."

This book is written for those who seek to experience the unique mountain trains, funiculars, cableways and steamers to some of the most impressive natural wonders. The entire transportation system is designed for easy connections and smooth traveling. Nature has provided the mountains, lakes and waterfalls producing exquisite scenery. And the Swiss people make it a reality, blending all the elements together to offer you new and memorable experiences with exceptional accommodations and restaurants.

We have been visiting this area for over 30 years. When we meet our friends, they ask, "What should we do?" "Where should we go?" This book is your answer to those questions - a guide to select trips in the Bernese Oberland. Whether you are young or old, with children or disabled, a hiker or one who likes to ride the mountain trains, this book will guide you through the Bernese Oberland.

Enjoy the area to the fullest: a mountain embrace, a peaceful sunset on a lake, an unforgettable ride on a mountain train, a quiet walk with a breathtaking view followed by a satisfying meal and a glass of the local wine.

Have a great time!

INTRODUCTION

The Bernese Oberland is a 60-mile long formidable wall of snowcapped mountains jutting thousands of feet into the sky, stretching for 30 miles to the east and 30 miles to the west of Interlaken. Below the mountains are green valleys, misty waterfalls and blue lakes. Many say this is the most beautiful part of the Alps that extend from Austria to France.

There is no other place like it in the world. There are higher mountains, larger lakes and deeper valleys elsewhere. Yet, this is the most easily traveled and accessible mountain area anywhere. In fact, this particular area of the Bernese Oberland just south of Interlaken has over five lakes, many waterfalls and 18 snow-covered peaks over 10,000 feet. Mountain trains, cableways, funiculars take you high into the mountains, where you can walk, hike or just relax. Steamers travel the beautiful lakes. In a few hours, you can be at 11,000 feet, riding a cog rail train up inside the mountain in complete comfort.

In the middle of this vast wall of mountains stands the Jungfrau Massif: the Eiger, Mönch and Jungfrau. This is one of the most impressive mountain ranges in the world.

The Jungfrau Massif makes its own weather. As the weather changes so does the character of the mountains. Just as you are

Interlaken circa 1880

always aware of the weather, so you are always aware of the splendor of the mountains and, yes, the silence. There is a peace and quiet in the mountains regardless of the weather.

Stories of the incredible beauty of the Bernese Oberland began to emerge from travelers to the area in the 1700 and 1800's. The English and the Germans were the first visitors to acclaim the grandeur of the region. The English became particularly fond of the area and many spent their summers in Interlaken and the villages of Grindelwald, Mürren, Wengen and Kandersteg. To this day, you will see many delightful English "tea rooms" in the towns and villages. As a result, many of the Swiss people speak English.

The Swiss saw the potential for attracting tourists to the area, and undertook the building of trains, cableways, steamers, hotels and inns to cater to their needs. Access to the mountains was made possible with the cog railway first built in the area in 1890. By the beginning of the century, all the major mountain trains were operating with the exception of the Jungfrau Bahn, a feat completed in 1912. The Jungfrau Bahn travels from Kleine Scheidegg to Eigergletscher, then climbs inside the 4½ mile tunnel through the Eiger, Mönch and to the Jungfraujoch. The electrified cog railway made it possible to climb the high mountains with ease in the Bernese Oberland, "the playground of Europe." This may well have been the beginning of the tourist industry in Switzerland.

In his book *A Tramp Abroad,* Mark Twain wrote of his journey by carriage in August 1878 from Luzern over the Brünig Pass to Brienz and on to Interlaken. After a short stay in Interlaken, he continued on to Kandersteg and then, with a guide, crossed over the Gemmi Pass (7616 ft). In those days it was the only route across the 60-mile

Interlaken circa 1880

wall of mountains to the Valais. It was a strenuous trip and took several days to complete. Today, it is just a few hours by train. Or it can be a delightful one-day excursion with trains, buses, a ride on the cable car and a 3½ hour walk over the pass. A day you will remember.

It was not until the end of the last century, with the arrival of the railroad and steam locomotive, that people could travel from all over Europe to the Bernese Oberland with ease and comfort. The early steam trains could operate only in the summer months in the mountains. Beginning in 1909, the trains were electrified and operated year-round. This made winter sports practical and heralded the start of downhill skiing.

Sir Arnold Lund introduced downhill skiing in the early 1900's, and Wengen was the site of the first downhill race from the Lauberhorn in 1921. This was the beginning of competitive skiing as we know it today.

Soon after World War II, with the advent of jet aircraft, visitors came from all over the world to witness the striking beauty of the Bernese Oberland. The Swiss built additional hotels and restaurants to take care of their many guests.

Today, people fly to Europe for business or vacation, which offers an excellent opportunity to include a visit to the Bernese Oberland. For example, if you happen to end the week in Paris on a Friday afternoon, you can take the TGV train to Bern and be in Interlaken that evening, ready to explore the mountains, lakes and forests the next morning. Or, if you fly into Zürich in the morning, you can be in the mountains that afternoon.

There is a different mood and tempo in the Bernese Oberland. It has a quieter pace. The people are friendly and courteous, and cleanliness abounds everywhere. There is always a restaurant and toilet, WC (water closet) as it is sometimes called, even in the most remote mountain locations.

Much of the beauty of the area can be seen from the train, cable car, bus or steamer. Very little walking is necessary. However, if you want to walk and hike, many additional vistas are opened up to you. Some of the most beautiful walks take less than two hours and can be done with "street shoes". Walking shoes are preferred and, for a few walks, lightweight hiking boots are recommended.

The Bernese Oberland offers you a full range of activities from mountain trains, steamers, walks - or a perfect setting for a quiet afternoon.

PLANNING YOUR TRIP

BEST TIME TO GO

Any time in the spring, summer, fall or winter is a good time to be in the Bernese Oberland. Each season has its own special attractions and advantages. The flowers in the springtime blanket the Alps. In the late fall, it is drier, cooler and some of the funiculars, cableways and lake steamers are shut down for annual maintenance. It is a very peaceful and quiet time to be in this area.

The summer is ideal, school is out and everybody is on vacation. You will find, however, long lines at many of the most popular mountain trains, funiculars and cableways during July and August, the High Season. This is also the sunniest time.

With children, we believe it is best to go in June, when the flowers are blooming and there are fewer people. Everything is operating from the first week in June until the middle of October.

Many people prefer to go to the Bernese Oberland during September and early October. All the trains, funiculars, cableways and steamers are operating, and there are not so many visitors. The weather is generally dry, sunny and warm. It is a beautiful time of year to be in the mountains and on the lakes.

Sometimes the snow doesn't melt until late June at the higher elevations, and your walks may be restricted. Snow may start again in late September, but even then you can do most walks; the first snowfall doesn't last long on the trails.

The spectacular high elevation trips - the Jungfrau and the Schilthorn - are open all year, as are the mountain villages of Wengen, Mürren, Grindelwald and Kandersteg.

We are talking about the Alps in the spring, summer and fall. The Bernese Oberland is probably best known for the winter months and skiing under ideal conditions - a winter paradise.

Again, any time of the year the Bernese Oberland has its special attractions and can lead to a rewarding experience.

> In planning your trip, contact the **Swiss National Tourist Office** (see General Information) for brochures and maps on the particular towns and areas you plan to visit. They can provide you with a wealth of information regarding lodging, restaurants, local activities, timetables, package tours, etc. Don't leave home without contacting them.

WEATHER

The Bernese Oberland forms a barrier between the north and the south and produces its own local variations in the weather. Sometimes, it is unsettled and changing. Other times, there will be a week of beautiful warm, sunny weather or a week of light rain. From May to October, you can encounter warm, sunny days to cool, wet days. The elevation also has a great deal to do with the weather. For every 300 feet of altitude increase, you can expect a drop of 1°F. in temperature.

In the summer, most mornings are clear and sunny. Around midday, however, you will find clouds beginning to form around the mountain tops, sometimes resulting in partly cloudy afternoons or brief showers. This generally is a sign of continued good weather for the next few days. This is another reason to plan your mountain trips in the mornings.

Before planning a trip to the high elevations like the Jungfrau or Schilthorn, check the weather the afternoon before at the Tourist Office. Check again early the next morning before your departure. These are expensive trips and well worth the money, but should be done only in good weather.

You will hear people talk about the "Föhn." This is a warm, dry wind off the northern face of the mountains. Generally, you will have clear skies for a day or two followed by some rain.

RAINY DAY ACTIVITIES

There always is the possibility of rainy days. While you will not want to do the high elevation trips, there are other rewarding trips such as the lake steamers and mountain trains. With a raincoat and umbrella, you can explore **Interlaken** and the mountain villages of **Grindelwald**, **Wengen**, **Mürren** and **Kandersteg**.

An excellent rainy day activity is to take the train to Lauterbrunnen, then walk (or ride the bus) up the Lauterbrunnen Valley to the **Trümmelbach Waterfalls** ☎(036-55-32-32). The Trümmelbach drains the mighty glacier waters from the Eiger, Mönch and Jungfrau. Up to 5,000 gallons of water a second roar and thunder down the 60-foot Falls inside the mountain. The Falls are illuminated and accessible by tunnel lift. Another alternative is a visit to the **St. Beatus Caves** ☎(036) 41-16-43), a 10-minute ride on the bus, or take the steamer from Interlaken. The Caves were inhabited by cave dwellers thousands of years ago and offer a wide variety of stalactites and limestone formations. Or consider an excursion to **Bern** (page 73) where the covered arcades provide not only protection from the rain but a delightful sightseeing and shopping opportunity.

HOW TO GET THERE

In planning your trip to the Continent, schedule a few days or a week in the Bernese Oberland to explore the incredible mountains, lakes and valleys.

You are only hours away if you are in London, Paris, Amsterdam, Frankfurt or Milan. The distances in Europe are very short. In a few hours, you can be at your destination in the Bernese Oberland.

If you fly into Zürich or Geneva, take one of the clean, fast trains. Riding the train is an experience. Car rentals are expensive and not very useful in the mountains; the car will be parked most of the time. If you are driving, when you arrive in the area we suggest you park the car and ride the mountain trains, cableways and steamers.

This part of Switzerland, the Bernese Oberland, is easily reached by train or car. A visitor should consider using the trains, not only because of the excellent service - comfort, cleanliness and speed - but also because of the environment.

There are **four rail routes to Interlaken**, the center of the Bernese Oberland:

The **first** and fastest service from Northern Switzerland, France and Germany comes through Bern. This includes through-train service from Amsterdam and Cologne. If you are traveling from Zürich, it is a 2½ hour trip via Bern to Interlaken.

If you have an extra 30 minutes, you should consider the **second** more scenic route to Interlaken from Zürich via Luzern and over the Brünig Pass. Take the train from Zürich to Luzern, then change to the train to Interlaken. This passes the Vierwaldstättersee (Lake of Four Cantons), also called Lake of Luzern. This is a beautiful trip with views of Mt. Pilatus, the Sarnen See, continuing over the Brünig Pass to Meiringen, Brienz and on to Interlaken.

The **third** route comes from the South, Italy, the Valais and Brig. You will travel through the nine-mile long Lötschberg rail tunnel. The first stop after the tunnel is Kandersteg, with a change of trains in Spiez for the short run into Interlaken.

The **fourth** route is from Montreux on Lake Geneva. This is a beautiful three hour scenic ride through the mountains and Gstaad, with a change of trains at Zweisimmen (where the two Simmen rivers come together) and another change at Spiez before continuing on to Interlaken.

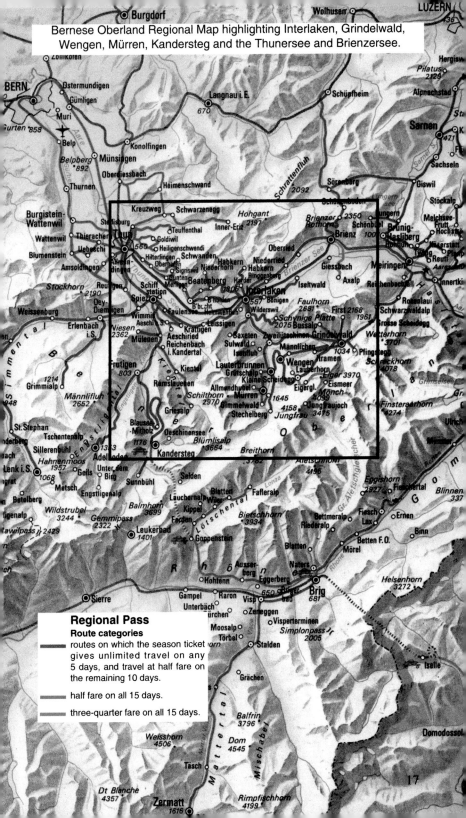

Bernese Oberland Regional Map highlighting Interlaken, Grindelwald, Wengen, Mürren, Kandersteg and the Thunersee and Brienzersee.

Regional Pass

Route categories

routes on which the season ticket gives unlimited travel on any 5 days, and travel at half fare on the remaining 10 days.

half fare on all 15 days.

three-quarter fare on all 15 days.

17

If you are coming from outside Switzerland, the Eurailpass is valid only as far as Interlaken. For the mountain trains beyond Interlaken, you can purchase individual tickets for each trip. Or, from a convenience and cost-effective standpoint, you can purchase a **Bernese Oberland Regional Pass** for five unlimited travel days, during a 15-day period, on mountain railways, cableways, funiculars, steamers and buses. There is an extra fare for the trip to the Jungfrau and the Schilthorn, but it's well worth it on a clear day.

The **Swiss Pass** is valid everywhere in Switzerland, including the mountain trains as far as Grindelwald, Mürren and Wengen, with a discount on many other mountain trains and lifts.

Another nice thing about traveling in Switzerland is the **"Fly-Rail Baggage"** system. Rail passengers have the unique opportunity of checking their baggage from Zürich or Geneva Airports directly to their Swiss destination for a small fee. A great convenience!

Train along the Thunersee

HOW TO USE THE GUIDE

To assist you in planning your trips, we first describe the area in terms of the Mountains, Lakes and types of Transportation:

- Mountains
- Mountain Trains
- Cableways
- Funiculars
- Lakes
- Steamers
- Walks

A map identifies the location of each of the Ten Trips and four all-day Excursions.

Depending on the transportation and the amount of walking you want to do, the next two charts identify the Ten Trips with the mountains, lakes and transportation.

This is followed with a description of each trip, including elevation, how much walking is required and how long it takes. A trip map is included to show the route of each of the Ten Trips. Where appropriate, we have listed optional routes to include a walk or an alternate train ride to capture the beauty of the area.

After reviewing the list of trips, you may want to switch the order around to suit your individual preferences. On some days, you will want to do two trips - the mountains in the morning and a steamer on the lake in the afternoon. An important factor is the weather. Sunny days are preferred, but partly cloudy weather is still good for many trips.

DS Lötschberg on the Brienzersee

The mountains create their own weather, so it is important to check the forecast in the evening to plan the next day. It is best to plan an alternate trip, in the event the weather is not favorable for your first choice trip. Then, first thing in the morning, check the weather and make your final decision as to your trip plan. Pack a picnic lunch, or plan to have lunch in one of the mountain restaurants or on a lake steamer, and be off for a delightful experience.

For those who wish to engage in more energetic walks or hikes, there are many excellent guidebooks on the more strenuous trails in the area. (See General Information) A word of caution. Don't plan to do a strenuous hike the first few days you are in the mountains. Get acclimated. Start with some of the easier walks and work up to the strenuous hikes.

Typically, a visitor will spend less than one week in the area the first time. This is a small area, but offers the greatest variety of activities and scenery imaginable. On future visits, you will want to stay longer and explore the many other trips and excursions.

Whether you are spending one day or ten days in the Bernese Oberland, it can be one of the great experiences of your life - to ride mountain trains and steamers and savor the food and wine.

Use this book as a personal guide. It will be the start of a love affair with the "most beautiful part of the world."

For convenience and because of Interlaken's close proximity to everything, all times, distances and changes in elevation are shown from Interlaken.

All the trips can be done easily from **Grindelwald**, **Wengen**, **Mürren** or **Kandersteg**, if you are staying in one of these mountain villages. Some trips will take a little more time, some less, but they all can be done in less than a day. We have chosen **Wengen** as our headquarters and have experienced all the trips from that beautiful mountain village.

The Eiger, Mönch, Jungfrau from Schynige Platte

MOUNTAINS

The snowcapped mountains of the Bernese Oberland are some of the most impressive in the world. There are other great mountain ranges, but none are so accessible while maintaining their natural beauty. This ice-encrusted wall of mountains stretches for sixty miles along the southern edge of the canton of Bern. The midpoint of this range is south of Interlaken.

Not only are the mountains easy to reach but, within a few hours travel time, you can be at 11,000 feet, playing in the snow or looking out over the Aletsch glacier, the longest in Europe. This can all be done in comfort by mountain train.

The only passage through this wall of mountains is the nine-mile long Lötschberg tunnel, accessible from Kandersteg and Brig in the Valais. In addition, there is an easy walk from Kandersteg, with the assist of cable cars, across the Gemmi Pass, along the Daubensee to Leukerbad in the Valais.

There are many mountain tops, easily accessible, that have beautiful panoramic views of the mountains and the lakes. One of the better views is from the **Niesen** (7747 ft) on the Thunersee, accessible by funicular.

For those who appreciate an old-fashioned steam locomotive pushing a train, the only steam cog train in Switzerland still chugs up to the **Rothorn Kulm** (7433 ft) from Brienz. From here, you have a superb view of the Brienzersee below and the snowcapped mountains to the south.

Then, of course, there is the view from the **Schilthorn** (9744 ft), accessible via a four-stage cableway from the Lauterbrunnen Valley, where one can survey the snow-covered wall of mountains to the south.

The grandest and highest view of all is from the **Jungfrau Sphinx** (11,723 ft), accessible by mountain trains from Lauterbrunnen or Grindelwald. This is Europe's highest railway, completed in 1912, and is one of the great mountain experiences.

In this enchanting area, one is surrounded by some of the most impressive mountains accessible by cog train or cableway. If you want to walk and hike, additional areas are opened up to you, such as a sunrise view of the Alps from the top of the **Faulhorn** (8794 ft), just north of Grindelwald. This is a fairly strenuous hike and will be a most memorable one.

Nowhere is it possible to experience the majesty of the mountains so easily or be as totally embraced by them as in the Bernese Oberland.

Walking on a mountain path

Mountain train to Schynige Platte (SPB)

MOUNTAIN TRAINS

A **mountain train** is a narrow gauge railroad that at various times uses a cog rail or rack and pinion to provide the necessary traction to climb the steep mountain grades.

The six major mountain trains in the area are:

Jungfrau Bahn	**JB**
Brienzer Rothorn Bahn	**BRB**
Bernese Oberland Bahn	**BOB**
Wengernalp Bahn	**WAB**
Bergbahnen Lauterbrunnen-Mürren	**BLM**
Schynige Platte Bahn	**SPB**

Five of the six mountain trains in the Jungfrau area were operating at the turn of the century. The sixth train, the **Jungfrau Bahn (JB)**, Europe's highest railroad, opened in 1912. It took nine years to build the 4½ mile tunnel up through the Eiger, Mönch to the Jungfraujoch (11,333 ft). It takes just under one hour to make the trip from Kleine Scheidegg to the top on the electrified train. One of the advantages of the JB is that it travels inside the mountain, leaving the outside unscarred.

As you look at the Jungfrau Massif covered with snow and ice, you would never know that a train was running in a tunnel moving people up and down through the mountain.

Since 1912, no new trains have been built in the area. All the trains have been modernized and are electric, with the exception of the **Brienzer Rothorn Bahn (BRB)** which runs from the village of Brienz (1873 ft) on the Brienzersee to the **Rothorn Kulm** (7433 ft). Most of the BRB trains have the old original steam locomotives from the 1890's. Some new, more powerful steam locomotives are being added to the line. The train can be seen as you arrive in Brienz by boat or by train. It takes 55 minutes to chug up and around the mountain to the top of the Rothorn. At several points, the train appears to be hanging on the side of the cliffs.

The primary train in the Jungfrau area is the **Bernese Oberland Bahn (BOB)**. The BOB is affectionately known as the "Best of Bahn's" because of its excellent, friendly service. It runs from Interlaken Ost (East) (1856 ft) to Grindelwald (3390 ft) and another section to Lauterbrunnen (2686 ft). The first stop is Wilderswil (1916 ft), a five-minute run, and the next stop is Zweilütschinen (2139 ft), nine minutes away. This is where the two Lütschinen rivers come together, the Schwarze (black) Lütschine from Grindelwald and the Weisse (white) Lütschine from the Lauterbrunnen Valley. From here, the first section of the train goes on to Lauterbrunnen (9 minutes), and the rear section goes to Grindelwald (23 minutes). On the way to Grindelwald, you "pick up" the cog rail, the train slows and you can hear the cog engaging the rack, as the train climbs up the grade. This also occurs on the Lauterbrunnen section where you can hear the train pick up on the cog rail as it goes up the grade just before the Lauterbrunnen station. The BOB is the only mountain train with a First Class section.

Wengernalp Bahn

At Grindelwald, a popular Alpine village known for its glaciers, riders change to the **Wengernalp Bahn (WAB)**. This mountain train takes you up to Kleine Scheidegg (6770 ft). In just 40 minutes, the train climbs to the pass between the Lauterbrunnen Valley and Grindelwald. At Kleine Scheidegg, change trains to continue up to the Jungfraujoch (11,333 ft) on the JB. If you are not going up to the Jungfraujoch, have lunch at Kleine Scheidegg, then take the WAB down the other side of the mountain to Wengen and Lauterbrunnen in the valley. In Lauterbrunnen, take the BOB back to Interlaken Ost.

You can have a different train experience if you cross the street in Lauterbrunnen and take the **Bergbahnen Lauterbrunnen-Mürren (BLM)**. The first part of the ride takes you from Lauterbrunnen (2686 ft) to Grütschalp (4874 ft) on a funicular. This is an eight-minute ride straight up the mountain on the other side of the valley. At Grütschalp, a station known for its view of the Jungfrau, take the single electric train car to Mürren (5396 ft). This is a 14-minute ride with a stop halfway at Winteregg (5176 ft) to allow the train coming in the opposite direction from Mürren to pass. This little single car hugs the side of the mountain, passes through woods, fields and across streams before arriving at Mürren. If you sit on the left side of the car going to Mürren, you will have a spectacular and ever-changing view of the mountains.

There is still another mountain train, the **Schynige Platte Bahn (SPB)**. Catch this train at Wilderswil (1916 ft), just across the tracks from the BOB train station, and it takes you to the top at Schynige Platte (6488 ft) with its Alpine flower gardens and far ranging view. The train climbs through the forest and then above the trees to Schynige Platte and, in less than one hour, you have a sweeping view of the mountains and the lakes - one of the most scenic views in the area.

———————◆●◄———————

One of the advantages of the Bernese Oberland is that everything is synchronized. When you get off one train, in five to ten minutes the next train is ready to leave. In the middle of summer you may have to wait because of the many people, but most of the time you can catch the next train. Again, it is like having your own "train platform" or "train set" in the mountains. However, you can ride these trains and get on and off at each station as you wish, always to experience a spectacular view.

Very little walking is necessary to go from one train to another, which is convenient for families with young children, older members or the disabled. Also, there is ample room for a stroller or baby carriage on the trains.

One of the benefits of the train is that it takes you up the mountain with ease. From there, you can walk and then take another train or cable car down.

All of the mountain trains are privately owned and operated in conjunction with the **Swiss Federal Railways (SBB)**. Eurailpasses are not valid on the mountain trains.

Funicular from Interlaken to the Harder

FUNICULARS

A **Funicular** is a two-car lift connected by a single cable. As one car
goes up, the other car goes down. At the halfway point, the two cars
pass each other.

The five main funiculars in the area are:

Niesen Bahn	**NB**
Bergbahnen Lauterbrunnen-Mürren	**BLM**
Harder Bahn	**HB**
Giessbachsee Bahn	**GbB**
Thunersee Beatenberg Bahn	**TBB**

The **Niesen Bahn (NB)** funicular ride up the side of the Niesen is one
of the most spectacular. It was opened in 1910. It takes you up to the
pyramid-looking peak, Niesen Kulm (7747 ft), which is just south of
Spiez. You board the funicular at the Mülenen station, eight minutes
by train from Spiez. The funicular travels in two sections, ascending
5,474 feet, with an average grade of 54%. This ascent takes just under
30 minutes. At the top you will find a hotel and restaurant with an
unobstructed view of the Thunersee below and snowcapped Alps to the
south and southeast.

Another charming ride in the area is the **Bergbahnen Lauterbrunnen-
Mürren (BLM)** funicular deep in the Lauterbrunnen Valley. The
BLM starts from Lauterbrunnen (2686 ft) and ascends a 55% grade to
Grütschalp (4874 ft), a climb of 2,188 feet. You will see the
impressive Staubbach Falls, one of the highest in Europe. It takes 11
minutes to make the ascent. This funicular opened in 1891

and provides transportation from Lauterbrunnen to the mountain village of Mürren. Grütschalp is the first leg of the trip to Mürren. Here you change to the single car train that weaves along the side of the mountain before arriving at Mürren, 14 minutes later. This provides a spectacular, ever-changing view of the Jungfrau Massif.

The **Harder Bahn (HB)** funicular takes you to the Harder Station (4284 ft) overlooking Interlaken. It takes about 8 minutes to the top, with an average grade of 59% from the base station which is a six-minute walk from the Interlaken Ost rail station. From the restaurant and terrace, you have a panoramic view of the mountains, with Schynige Platte in the foreground. This is a great place for pastry, ice cream and coffee.

There is the short **Giessbachsee Bahn (GbB)** funicular that rises 295 feet from the dock at Giessbach on Lake Brienz, up to the Grand Hotel. This funicular was opened in 1879 as a water balance system and was converted to electric in 1912. It is an easy way to get from the lake to the Grand Hotel in four minutes.

On the north side of the Thunersee, at Beatenbucht (1876 ft), you will find the 5,589 foot long **Thunersee Beatenberg Bahn (TBB)** funicular. This takes you from the lake to the small station just west of Beatenberg (3680 ft) in 10 minutes. From the Beatenberg station continue on a 20-30 minute walk to the Niederhorn (6376 ft) chair lift. This provides another grand view of the lake and the Bernese Oberland.

Funicular from Lauterbrunnen to Grütschalp (BLM)

Schilthorn Cable Car (LSMS)

CABLEWAYS

A **Cableway** is an overhead endless cable. Cable cars are suspended from the cable to provide the transportation up the mountain.

The eight major cableways in the area are:

Luftseilbahn Stechelberg-Mürren-Schilthorn	**LSMS**
Gondolabahn Grindelwald-First	**GGF**
Luftseilbahn Wengen-Männlichen	**LWM**
Gondolabahn Grindelwald-Männlichen	**GGM**
Luftseilbahn Grindelwald-Pfingstegg	**LGP**
Luftseilbahn Kandersteg Sunnbühl-Gemmi	**LKSG**
Luftseilbahn Leukerbad-Gemmipass	**LLG**
Luftseilbahn Erlenbach Stockhorn	**LESt**

In recent years, the cable cars have become the most efficient way to transport people to distant mountain tops. The most famous is the **Luftseilbahn Stechelberg-Mürren-Schilthorn (LSMS)** to the top of the Schilthorn which opened in 1967. In four stages and 32 minutes, it takes you from Stechelberg (2985 ft) in the Lauterbrunnen Valley to the top of the Schilthorn (9744 ft), with changes in Gimmelwald, Mürren and Birg. The Schilthorn is one of the world's highest revolving restaurants. On a clear day, you have an unsurpassed view of the Bernese Oberland with the Jungfrau Massif to the east.

The newest gondola cableway is the **Gondolabahn Grindelwald-First (GGF)**. This is a six passenger gondola from Grindelwald (3390 ft) to First (7216 ft), a 20-minute ride to the top with no changes. You pass through two stations and can exit at either. At the top, First, there is a restaurant with sun deck, and an overall view of the Wetterhorn in the center and the Eiger and Jungfrau off to the right.

28

Another rewarding cable car ride is the **Luftseilbahn Wengen-Männlichen (LWM)**. It takes six minutes from Wengen (4180 ft) to Männlichen (7314 ft) with a spectacular view of the mountains and Lauterbrunnen Valley. This is the start of the beautiful walk to Kleine Scheidegg. Sometimes chamois are seen on the mountainside.

The longest gondola cableway, **Gondolabahn Grindelwald-Männlichen (GGM)** from Grindelwald (Grund) to Männlichen (7314 ft) is 4 miles long and a 30-minute ride. The Grund Station is approximately a half-mile from the center of Grindelwald.

Luftseilbahn Grindelwald-Pfingstegg (LGP) travels from Grindelwald to Pfingstegg (4562 ft) in four minutes. At Pfingstegg, there is a restaurant and a view of Grindelwald, situated in the basin below, with a close-up view of the Eiger. From here, there are several walks to the glaciers above Grindelwald.

Luftseilbahn Kandersteg Sunnbühl-Gemmi (LKSG) rises from just south of Kandersteg (3856 ft) to Sunnbühl (6359 ft) in 25 minutes, on your way to the Gemmi Pass, with some spectacular views. After a 3½ hour walk, with a stop at the Schwarenbach mountain hotel (6780 ft) about halfway, you arrive at the Gemmi Pass. Here, the **Luftseilbahn Leukerbad-Gemmipass (LLG)** cableway will take you down from the Gemmi Pass (7616 ft) to Leukerbad (4671 ft) in the Valais in five minutes. This is an all-day excursion from Interlaken.

Luftseilbahn Erlenbach Stockhorn (LESt) is accessible from the Simmentalbahn line from Spiez to Erlenbach. The cableway is a 15 minute walk from the Erlenbach rail station. The cable car takes you to the Stockhorn (7183 ft) in 15 minutes in two sections with a change at Chrindi (5386 ft). After a short climb, you are high above Thun and can look down the Thunersee to Interlaken. For those who like to fish, Hinterstockensee is a short distance from the Chrindi station. This is an all-day trip from Interlaken.

Cableway to Stockhorn with panorama of Alps

Aerial view of Thunersee and Interlaken

LAKES ~~~~

The five main lakes in the area are:

Thunersee
Brienzersee
Oeschinensee
Blausee
Bachalpsee

While the snowcapped mountains are the central point of the Bernese Oberland, there also are many beautiful lakes in the region. The lakes offer a change of pace that is quite different from the mountains.

The two largest lakes, the **Thunersee** (Lake of Thun) and the **Brienzersee** (Lake of Brienz), are separated by the two-mile long village of Interlaken (between the lakes). Originally, it was one long lake. Then, during pre-historic times, the Lütschine River to the south and the Lombach River to the north brought stone and sediment down from the mountains and filled in the area causing the lakes to separate. This created the "Bödeli", or the flat land, on which Interlaken is built.

The Aare river flows from the glaciers in the Grimsel Pass weaving its way down to the **BRIENZERSEE**. The Brienzersee is a wild mountain lake cradled between steep mountains. It is nine miles long and one-to-two miles wide. It is a cold, clear lake, 850 feet deep, with a light greenish tinge to the water. The old road and railroad are on the north side of the lake. You will see many small boats out on the lake with people fishing, and steamers sailing up and down the lake calling at the seven docks of the charming villages surrounding the lake.

Near Brienz at the far end of the lake is **Ballenberg**. This is the **Swiss Open Air Museum** of rural dwellings and lifestyles. There are 13 different regions of the country planned for in this park-like setting dating back to the l7th Century.

The **THUNERSEE** is a larger and more developed lake. It is 11 miles long and to the west of Interlaken. At the far end of the lake is the city of Thun, population 33,000. The lake is one-to two-miles wide and 712 feet deep. This is the more populated of the two lakes, with 14 villages with vineyards on the lake, and a road system that surrounds the lake. The railroad is on the south shore. Many steamers ply the lake in the summertime.

There is much history surrounding the Thunersee, with picturesque medieval castles at Spiez, Oberhofen, Hilterfingen and Thun. These castles have been turned into museums. The Thunersee is the fifth largest lake in Switzerland.

The **OESCHINENSEE** is high in the Kander valley, just outside of Kandersteg. The Blümlisalp towers above the lake and reflects its rugged mass in the clear blue water. The lake is easily reached by a slight downhill 30-minute walk from the chairlift that comes up from Kandersteg. Many people consider this to be the most beautiful of all Alpine lakes.

Another jewel is the crystal clear **BLAUSEE**, the deep blue lake north of Kandersteg. You can see the large alpine trout swimming in the lake. The Blausee, with a restaurant, terrace and trout farm, is a 10-minute bus ride south from Kandersteg or a 12-minute bus ride north from Frutigen.

The **BACHALPSEE** is another mountain lake cradled beneath the Faulhorn, just northeast of Grindelwald. It reflects the Wetterhorn and the Schreckhorn to the south. The lake is easily accessible on the path from the station at First (1½ hour walk).

Oberhofen on the Thunersee

Steamer on the Brienzersee

STEAMERS

The many steamers on the Thunersee and the Brienzersee are operated by the Thuner and Brienzersee Steamer Company. The steamer timetables are coordinated with the trains and buses, so that you can travel one way by steamer and return by train or bus.

In the middle of the last century, large paddle wheel steamers were carrying passengers up and down the Thunersee and the Brienzersee.

By 1872, one could travel from Thun to Brienz by steamer and train: the paddle steamer from Thun to Interlaken, then the Bödeli Bahn (train) across to the Brienzersee, and another steamer to Brienz. In the early days, the paddle steamers were the main transportation system around the lakes.

At the end of the 1800's, most of the railroads had been built and were the major link to the rest of Europe. This provided easy transportation into the area for visitors.

The steamers continue to serve the people living around the lakes, as well as the many visitors to the area.

One of the old elegant paddle steamers, the **DS Lötschberg**, built in 1914 and carrying 1000 passengers still operates on the Brienzersee. There are five other diesel powered "steamers" traveling the lake, with stops at ten ports or villages. It takes the steamers about 1½ hours (nine miles) from Interlaken to Brienz, with between six and eight port calls.

On the Thunersee, you have the newly reconditioned paddle steamer, the **DS Blümlisalp**, built in 1906. This grand old steamer was relaunched in 1992 and can carry 800 passengers. In addition to the paddle wheeler, there are 12 additional diesel powered "steamers" plying the 11-mile long lake. This is the largest of the two lakes, and there are 17 ports or villages on its shores. It takes a little over two hours to make the delightful trip from Interlaken to Thun, with 11-to-12 stops along the way.

The steamers leave about every hour and are a pleasant way to see the lake and the surrounding mountains. In addition, on many of the steamers, you can have a leisurely lunch or dinner. In the summer months, there are evening excursions on the lakes with dinner and dancing.

One of the enjoyable rewards of taking a steamer is to watch the sunset behind the mountains from the deck. Another advantage of taking the steamers is convenience. At Thun and Interlaken West on the Thunersee, and Brienz and Interlaken Ost on the Brienzersee, the dock or landing is next to the railway station. This makes it easy to go by steamer in one direction and return by train. Or, you can start out by steamer from Interlaken West on the Thunersee, then catch the train at Thun and continue on your journey to Bern and Zürich. You can do the same traveling to Luzern. Take the steamer from Interlaken Ost to Brienz, then hop the train to Luzern. This combination offers a very scenic trip.

DS Lötschberg Paddle Steamer

Wanderweg - Hiking Path

WALKS

When you think of the Bernese Oberland, you think of the Alps, walking and hiking. Books have been written about the many beautiful hikes in the area - uphill, downhill and across the mountains. (See General Information)

There are many outstanding walks that can be enjoyed by visitors to the higher elevations with walking shoes (or even street shoes). On some of the trails, you will see people with baby carriages and even high heel shoes (not recommended). There are level walks along the lakes and at the higher elevations. Each village has a range of easy walks.

Wherever you go in the Bernese Oberland, you will see people walking. It is a country of walkers. For an exhilarating "mountain experience", the trains, cable cars and funiculars will take you well above the permanent snowline among the giant peaks. Then start walking on one of the well marked trails. Every Kiosk (newsstand), bookstore and rail station has maps of the area. Also, most of the cableways, gondolas and chairlifts have brochures with maps for the asking.

You will find two kinds of walking routes in the Alps. A **"Wanderweg"** or walking route is an easy graded path through the hills or mountains. A **"Bergweg"** or mountain route is a more difficult path. The signs for the routes are painted in yellow and point the direction with the walking time. For the Bergweg, the yellow signpost pointer is marked with a white-red-white stripe. If there is no sign, you may see the route blazed with white-red-white painted on a rock to let you know you are still on the route.

The Swiss do not camp out with sleeping bags and tents. They experience the mountains in a more civilized way, staying in a chalet, apartment or hotel in a mountain village. Then, with a small day pack, they head out each morning by train or lift to walk a different path high up in the mountains, returning in the evening. They might stop along the way for a picnic or a meal at a mountain restaurant. On some of the longer and more strenuous hikes, they will spend the night at a mountain hotel or a Swiss Alpine Club (SAC) hut.

Whenever possible, to appreciate the ever-changing view, walk towards the mountains. Plan your outing so that you are facing the snowcapped mountain as you walk and keep looking up. You will see many people walking: youngsters, families and older people. Greet them in the Swiss tradition of **"Gruezi"** (Greetings), or **"Grüss Gott"** (Grace of God be with you). You may even pass cows, with their distinctive bells, on the trail. A walk will give you a different perspective of the Alps and reveal their true beauty.

On some of the more popular walks, you may find quite a few people. Do not try to escape from them. You are all there to experience the walk and the grandeur of the mountains. These are people like yourself, who want to experience the fresh air and beauty of the mountains and the ever changing scenery as they walk.

Discovering a new walk can be exciting. Always take along a map and begin exploring on your own. There is no need to feel apprehensive; you won't get lost. The majority of the walks are easy and can be done in a few hours or half a day. All the walks are well marked with signs. If the sign marks the town as a one hour walk, plan that it will take you 10 to 15 minutes longer, unless you are in good physical condition and don't plan to make any stops along the way. Again, the views are spectacular.

Wanderweg to First

Wengernalp Bahn to Kleine Scheidegg

TEN TRIPS

There are many things to do, places to visit, sights to see, in the Bernese Oberland. We have listed what we believe are the **ten best trips** that will give you the most enjoyment - the greatest satisfaction - beginning with number one, traveling up to the Jungfrau on a clear day. This is a journey to the highest railway station in Europe. If you have only one day in the Bernese Oberland, we recommend that you make this trip. From the top you can see the glaciers to the south, and the mountains and lakes to the north. The train ride up through the mountain is impressive.

After the Jungfrau, we have listed nine additional trips from which you can pick and choose. It may be a walk along the shore of the Brienzersee, a relaxed trip on one of the lake steamers, or a walk through the mountains. Select what interests you the most; they are all scenic and one is sure to fit your mood and the weather.

The map on the next page identifies the location of the **Ten Trips** and four all-day **Excursions**. On the following page is a **Ten Trip Planner** describing each trip in summary form. All the trips are great, so shuffle the order to suit your own desire.

After the **Ten Trip Planner**, the **Destination & Activity Locator** identifies each event by Trip and Page Number.

Each of the **Ten Trips** is then described in some detail with a map and suggested optional side trips.

Enjoy each trip!

AREA MAP LOCATING THE 10 TRIPS AND 4 EXCURSIONS

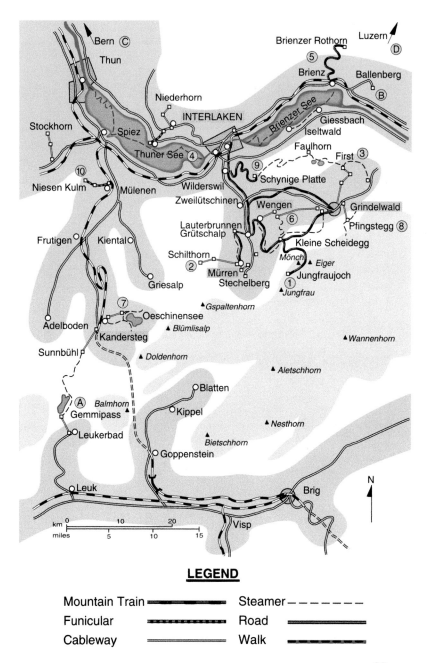

LEGEND

Mountain Train	Steamer
Funicular	Road
Cableway	Walk

TEN TRIP PLANNER

1. JUNGFRAU - COG TRAIN (Lauterbrunnen/Wengen/Grindelwald)
Station 11,333 Ft.   Half Day

2. SCHILTHORN - CABLEWAY (Lauterbrunnen/Mürren/Stechelberg)
Station 9,744 Ft.   Half Day

    Option A: Funicular/Train 15 Min. Walk

    Option B: Funicular 2 Hr. Walk

3. FIRST - GONDOLA (Grindelwald)
Station 7,216 Ft.   Half Day

    Option A: Easy 3 Hr. walk to Bachalpsee and return

    Option B: Easy 2 Hr. walk to Grosse Scheidegg

    Option C: 3 Hr. walk to Faulhorn

4. THUNERSEE - STEAMER (Interlaken)
Interlaken 1,856 Ft.   Half Day

    Option A: Half Day trip to the Niederhorn

5. BRIENZER ROTHORN - STEAM TRAIN (Brienz)
Station 7,433 Ft.   Half Day

    Option A: Steamer to Iseltwald, 2 Hr. walk to Giessbach

    Option B: Steamer to Giessbach

6. MÄNNLICHEN - CABLEWAY (Wengen)
Station 7,314 Ft.   Half Day   1½ Hr. Walk

    Option A: 2 Hr. walk to Wengen

    Option B: Train to Jungfrau (Trip #1)

7. OESCHINENSEE - CHAIRLIFT (Kandersteg)
Lake 5,225 Ft.   Half Day   1½ Hr. Walk

8. PFINGSTEGG - CABLEWAY (Grindelwald)
Station 4,562 Ft.   Half Day   3 Hr. Walk

9. SCHYNIGE PLATTE - COG TRAIN (Wilderwil)
Station 6,488 Ft.   Half Day

10. NIESEN - FUNICULAR (Mülenen)
Station 7,747 Ft.   Half Day

⋀⋀⋀	🚋	🚃	🚠	∼∼∼	⛴	🚶	TIME Hrs.
	●						5
●	●		●				4-5
●	●	●	●			●	5-6
●	●	●				●	4
●	●		●				4-5
●	●		●	●		●	7
●	●		●			●	7
●	●		●	●		●	8
				●	●		3-4
		●	●	●	●	●	3-4
●	●			●	●		4-5
				●	●	●	4-5
				●	●		3-4
●	●		●			●	4-5
●	●					●	6
●	●						6-7
●	●			●		●	4-5
●	●		●			●	4-5
●	●						4
●	●	●					4

DESTINATION & ACTIVITY LOCATOR

MOUNTAINS	TRIP	PAGE
Niesen	10	68
Brienzer Rothorn	5	56
Schilthorn	2	45
Jungfrau	1	42
Faulhorn	3	53
Männlichen	6	59
Schynige Platte	9	66
Pfingstegg	8	64
Gemmi Pass	A	70

MOUNTAIN TRAINS		
Jungfrau (JB)	1	42
Brienzer-Rothorn (BRB)	5	56
Wengernalp (WAB)	1,6	42,59
Mürren (BLM)	2	47
Schynige Platte (SPB)	10	66

FUNICULARS		
Niesen (NB)	8	68
Mürren (BLM)	2	47
Giessbach (GbB)	5	58
Beatenberg (TBB)	4	55

CABLEWAYS		
Schilthorn (LSMS)	2	45
First (GGF)	3	49
Männlichen (LWM)	6	59
Pfingstegg (LGP)	8	64
Sunnbühl (LKSG)	A	70
Gemmi Pass (LLG)	A	70

LAKES		
Thunersee	4	54
Brienzersee	5	56
Oeschinensee	7	62
Bachalpsee	3	51

STEAMERS		
Thunersee	4	54
Brienzersee	5	56

WALKS	TRIP	PAGE
⅃ * Männlichen-Kleine Scheidegg	6	59
* Grütschalp-Mürren	2	48
* First-Bachalpsee	3	51
* First-Faulhorn	3	53
First-Grosse Scheidegg	3	52
Iseltwald-Giessbach	5	57
Kandersteg-Oeschinensee	7	62
Pfingstegg-Stieregg	8	64
Gemmi-Sunnbühl	A	70

All of the walks listed above are great! We believe the four most beautiful walks in the Jungfrau area are those marked *.

There are countless walks worth exploring, such as the hike up into the Lauterbrunnen valley from Stechelberg to Obersteinberg.

———————➤●◄———————

DISTANCES FROM INTERLAKEN

The villages, mountains and lakes are relatively close together. The chart below displays the distances from Interlaken to the surrounding villages.

Wilderswil	3 km	2 miles
Zweilütschinen	8 km	5 miles
Lauterbrunnen	12 km	7 miles
Spiez	14 km	9 miles
Wengen	16 km	10 miles
Brienz	16 km	10 miles
Trümmelbach	16 km	10 miles
Mürren	18 km	11 miles
Stechelberg	20 km	12 miles
Grindelwald	20 km	12 miles
Ballenberg	23 km	14 miles
Thun	26 km	16 miles
Kandersteg	41 km	25 miles
Bern	54 km	34 miles
Grimsel Pass	68 km	42 miles
Luzern	70 km	43 miles
Brig	117 km	73 miles
Montreux	121 km	75 miles
Zürich	131 km	81 miles
Geneva	205 km	127 miles

1. JUNGFRAU

Europe's highest train station, Jungfraujoch (11,333 ft), with a train ride of unsurpassed views of the surrounding mountains, glaciers, valleys and lakes.

Round-Trip Time from Interlaken 5 Hours (½day)		
Highest Elevation:	11,723 Feet	Sphinx
Change in Elevation:	9,867 Feet	from Interlaken
Walking: very little required		
Best in clear, sunny weather	Information ☎(036) 55-10-22	

You can journey up into the very soul of the **Jungfrau**, be a part of it and experience its grandeur and majesty. You will feel the force of the mountain as you look over the glaciers and snow-covered peaks to the south and the hills and lakes to the north.

Plan to take the highest railway in Europe to the **Jungfraujoch** (11,333 ft) for an experience you will never forget. It is best to take an early train, when the weather is good and crowds are small. It takes about 2½ hours from Interlaken (1856 ft) to travel to the top. You will change trains twice on this scenic route.

Take the BOB train from **Interlaken Ost** to **Lauterbrunnen**, the end of the line. It takes about 25 minutes, with two stops along the way, as the train moves up the Lauterbrunnen Valley with mountains on both sides. When you arrive at Lauterbrunnen (2686 ft), cross the

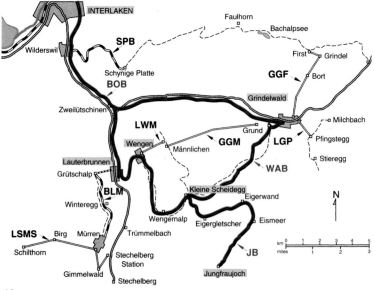

platform to the WAB train which will take you up to **Kleine Scheidegg** (6770 ft). This is an all-cog railway and will make the climb up the mountain in about 45 minutes. The train stops at **Wengen** (4180 ft). This is one of the prettiest mountain resorts in the area. There are no cars in the town. The only way up is to ride the train or walk. Wengen is one of the best places to view a sunset with the red Alpine glow on the Jungfrau. From Wengen, you have a view of the Jungfrau (13,647 ft), with the Breithorn (12,415 ft) and the Tschingelhorn (11,733 ft) gleaming with their snow cover to the right.

As the train leaves Wengen and climbs up through the pastures and woods, you will see the village of **Mürren** (5396 ft) on the other side of the Lauterbrunnen Valley. The train will make a brief stop at **Wengernalp** (6143 ft), where you will have a superb view of the enormous Jungfrau in front of you. In ten minutes you are at Kleine Scheidegg, the end of the line. This is the pass between Grindelwald and Lauterbrunnen. After walking to the south side of the station, take the **Jungfraubahn (JB)** for the incredible ride up inside the mountains to the Jungfraujoch.

The train runs straight up into the mountain for ten minutes to **Eigergletscher** (7609 ft). This part of the railway was completed in 1898. The train heads into the 4½ mile tunnel at the Eiger. Forty minutes later, after burrowing up through the Eiger and the Mönch, the train arrives at the **Jungfraujoch**. It will make a short stop at **Eigerwand** (9397 ft). Look through the large windows in the north face of the Eiger and see Kleine Scheidegg and Grindelwald below. While the Eigerwand station was completed inside the Eiger in 1903, the north face (Nordwand) was not successfully climbed until 1938.

The train then makes a ninety degree turn inside the Eiger and arrives at **Eismeer** (10,360 ft). This station was completed in 1905. You are now halfway through the tunnel. As you look out the large windows carved through the rock, over the Fiescher glacier, you will

Majestic view of the Jungfrau

see the gleaming Schreckhorn mountain. Now, with two miles left to travel mostly through the Mönch, the train continues to climb and arrives at the Jungfraujoch station (11,333 ft), the end of the line. There is a complete underground complex at the Jungfraujoch with restaurants, ice palace, ski school and mountain dogs. This station opened August 1, 1912. You will want to go out on the snow-covered plateau where there is a large Swiss flag and a wonderful view of the green-covered mountains to the north. Also be sure to take the elevator to the **Sphinx** (11,723 ft) for the highest panoramic view of the surrounding mountains and lakes. A sight to behold.

From the restaurant, on the back side of the mountain, look south to the 16-mile long Aletsch glacier, the largest in Europe. This feeds into the Rhône River in the Valais and from there to Lake Geneva and the Mediterranean. The snow and ice from the north side of the Jungfrau thunder down through the Trümmelbach Falls to the Weisse Lütschine River and on to the Brienzersee and the Aare River, and then to the Rhine. At 11,000 feet, you won't want to do any running around. After lunch, take the JB down to Kleine Scheidegg. At this point, you may elect to return via the village of **Grindelwald** (3390 ft) on the other side of the pass. If you take this route, you will ride under the north face of the Eiger and descend into the Grindelwald bowl, surrounded by three massive mountains to the south: the Eiger, the Mättenberg and the dominant Wetterhorn.

Grindelwald is known for the glaciers to the south and east of town. It is one of the premier resorts in the area. From the Grindelwald station, you change to the BOB train to **Interlaken**. It takes about 40 minutes. Total time for the round-trip, with lunch at the Jungfraujoch, is about five hours.

For the trip up the Jungfrau, take warm clothing, sun lotion, hat, gloves and sunglasses. It is cold at the top, even with the sun.

Sphinx and Aletsch Glacier

2. SCHILTHORN

One of the longest cableways in the Alps rises in four sections from the Lauterbrunnen Valley to the Schilthorn, high above Mürren, with a panorama of the Bernese Oberland.

Round-Trip Time from Interlaken 4-5 Hours (½day)		
Highest Elevation:	9,744 feet	Schilthorn
Change in Elevation:	7,888 feet	from Interlaken
Walking: very little required (via Stechelberg)		
Best in clear, sunny weather	Information	☎(036) 23-14-44

Option A: Funicular/Train   15 Minute Easy Walk
Funicular from Lauterbrunnen to Grütschalp, then a 20-minute train ride to Mürren and a 15-minute walk through town to the Schilthorn Cable Car.

Option B: Funicular/Walk   2 Hour Easy Walk
Funicular from Lauterbrunnen to Grütschalp, then an easy walk to Mürren.

Options A and B are two of the most rewarding train rides/walks in the Alps. If you only want a 15-minute walk through the picturesque village of Mürren, we recommend you select Option A.

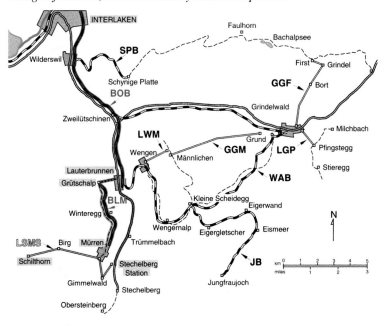

Jungfrau Massif from the Schilthorn

The **Schilthorn** provides a memorable westerly view of the Jungfrau Massif with an extended panorama of the world-class mountains of the Bernese Oberland. This cableway has the highest ascent in Switzerland and climbs 6,898 feet in four sections, with changes in **Gimmelwald** (4484 ft), **Mürren** (5396 ft), **Birg** (8780 ft), to the top of the **Schilthorn** (9744 ft). The ride up from **Stechelberg** in the Lauterbrunnen Valley takes 35 minutes.

The cableway opened in 1967, and the facilities at the top were expanded in 1990 to take care of the increased number of visitors. There are two restaurants, a self-service and the renowned Piz Gloria, a rotating restaurant. The Piz Gloria takes 50 minutes to rotate 360° with a full panoramic view of the area. Both restaurants have excellent menus.

The most popular route to the **Schilthorn**, and the one used by the tour buses, is via **Stechelberg** by bus or car. If you go by train, take the BOB from **Interlaken Ost** to **Lauterbrunnen**. Change to the yellow Postal Bus (PTT), several paces from the Lauterbrunnen station. Take the bus to the Stechelberg cable car station, a 10-15 minute ride up the valley. Here you catch the cable car to **Gimmelwald**, which takes 5 minutes. This is the first of four sections to the Schilthorn. At Gimmelwald change to the second section for the 5-minute ride to the village of **Mürren,** where you have a 5-minute connection to **Birg**. This is the longest section and takes 13 minutes. The final section from Birg to the Schilthorn takes only 4 minutes but provides a spectacular view. The total time from **Interlaken** to the top via Stechelberg is about 1½ hours, without any waiting and, with an hour at the summit, it is approximately a four-hour trip (half day).

OPTION A: Funicular/Train   15 Minute Easy Walk
Lauterbrunnen-Grütschalp-Mürren

The most scenic route to the **Schilthorn** is by way of **Grütschalp**. The funicular/train will take about 45 minutes and requires a 15-minute walk through the charming village of **Mürren,** from the train station at the north end to the cableway at the south end.

We recommend this scenic train ride along the side of the mountain to **Mürren**. It provides a continually changing view of the snow-covered peaks. Sit on the left side of the train for an unobstructed panorama. Well worth doing!

When you exit the BOB train in **Lauterbrunnen** (2686 ft), end of the line, walk north a few steps and cross the street to the **Lauterbrunnen-Mürren (BLM)** funicular. The funicular takes 11 minutes to ascend 2,188 feet to **Grütschalp** (4874 ft).

A single car train will be waiting to take you to **Mürren** (5396 ft), 2½ miles south, along the side of the mountain. The train ride takes 14 minutes. This is one of the shortest and most scenic train rides in the Alps. At the Mürren station, you need to walk 10-15 minutes to the south through the picturesque village to catch the cable car up the **Schilthorn**. **Mürren** is a delightful village for browsing, with excellent restaurants for lunch or tea.

Train from Grütschalp to Mürren (BLM)

47

OPTION B: Funicular/Walk   2 Hour Easy Walk
Lauterbrunnen-Grütschalp-Mürren

This is one of the most spectacular walks in the Alps. Take the funicular from **Lauterbrunnen** to **Grütschalp** (4874 ft). Then walk 2½ miles to **Mürren** (5396 ft) which will take approximately 1½ hours. The trail begins to the right as you leave the Grütschalp station. The pathway winds through woods, pastures filled with a colorful array of Alpine plants including yellow crocuses and blue gentians, and crosses several streams. You will be walking into the mountains so keep looking up. The pathway ascends a total of 522 feet. At the halfway point (1¼ miles), you will pass the **Winteregg** station (5176 ft). If you signal the train, it will stop and take you the rest of the way to **Mürren**. There will be people of all ages on the trail, including children and, at times, baby carriages. We suggest you wear walking shoes or lightweight hiking boots. Street shoes will do in a pinch. Enjoy one of the most beautiful walks. When you reach the Mürren rail station, you have an opportunity to use the facilities. Then continue on through the village. You only have another 10-15 minutes to the cable car for the return to Stechelberg and the bus back to Lauterbrunnen.

Many people take half a day to do this walk to **Mürren**, stopping at the restaurant at **Winteregg** for lunch, or carry a picnic lunch to eat along the way.

If you want to do the two-hour walk to **Mürren** and the cableway up to the **Schilthorn** in one day, reverse the order. Do the cableway to the Schilthorn in the morning when the weather is more predictable, then walk back from **Mürren** to **Grütschalp**.

Walk from Grütschalp to Mürren

3. FIRST

One of the longest gondola rides, north of Grindelwald, with outstanding views of the snowcapped Wetterhorn, Schreckhorn and the Eiger.

Round-Trip Time from Interlaken 4-5 hours (½ day)		
Highest Elevation:	7,216 feet	First
Change in Elevation:	5,360 feet	from Interlaken
Walking: very little required (10-15 minutes thru Grindelwald)		
Best on a clear, sunny day	Information ☎ (036) 53-36-38	

There are three beautiful walks from First:

Option A: Bachalpsee   **3 Hour Easy Walk Round-Trip**

Option B: Grosse Scheidegg   **2 Hour Easy Walk**

Option C: Faulhorn   **3 Hour Fairly Strenuous Hike**

The gondola cableway from **Grindelwald** to **First** recently replaced the longest chairlift in Europe. It operates in three sections. You can ride the six-person gondola all the way to the top station at **First** without any changes. Or you can ride up to **Bort** (5150 ft) or **Grindel** (6412 ft) and get off if you wish to walk part of the way up or down.

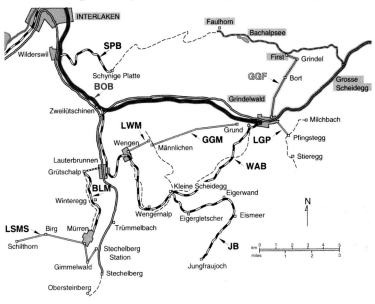

The gondola travels 3½ miles in about 20 minutes. During that time, you ascend 3,826 feet.

From **Interlaken Ost** take the BOB train to **Grindelwald**, then an easy 15-20 minute walk through town to the **Gondolabahn Grindelwald-First (GGF).** Follow the main street to the east. You can't miss the Gondolabahn, which will be on your left, up a few paces from the street. You will take the gondola up over green pastures and pine trees to the First Station. The translation for **First** is **"mountain ridge."**

At **First** (7216 ft), you have an excellent restaurant with a sun terrace and a panoramic view of the snowcapped Wetterhorn, Schreckhorn, Fiescherhorn, Eiger, Jungfrau to the south. To the east, you can see the path to Grosse Scheidegg Pass (6432 ft) and to the west, Kleine Scheidegg (6770 ft). Below, in the basin surrounded by the mountains, is the glacier village of **Grindelwald** (3390 ft).

Aerial view of Grindelwald looking south

OPTION A: To Bachalpsee   3 Hour Easy Walk Round-Trip

From **First** (7216 ft), you have the opportunity to walk to **Bachalpsee** (7429 ft), two small mountain lakes on the trail to the **Faulhorn**. These are some of the most photographed lakes in Switzerland, and the walk to the lakes takes a little over an hour. It is an easy ascent of 213 feet. This area is covered with an abundant array of flowers in the early summer.

When you leave the station at First, take the path down and to the left, following the trail signs to **Bachalpsee** and the **Faulhorn**. You will then climb over some large flat stones on a well-worn trail and cross over several small streams. Along the trail is a shelter hut. A short distance later, you will arrive at the two lakes that form the Bachalpsee. Here is another small hut and, to the north, you can see the Faulhorn with the white mountain hotel perched high on the side near the top.

After exploring the lake, and perhaps a picnic and a few pictures, you will want to walk back to the First station. Again, you are walking facing the mountains. Sometimes you can hear the roar of an avalanche and see the snow pluming upward on the Wetterhorn. This is a great walk with children.

It is an easy walk back on the well-traveled path. Be sure you are back to catch the last gondola down at 5:30 p.m.

Bachalpsee

OPTION B: To Grosse Scheidegg   2 Hour Easy Walk

From **First** (7216 ft), you can see **Grosse Scheidegg** (6432 ft) to the east and much of the trail. It is an easy downhill walk in the open. You will descend 784 feet. The trail hugs the side of the mountain. About halfway, you will pass some buildings at **Oberläger** as you continue on your way.

The Wellhorn will be in front of you until the last part of your walk, when you will be walking towards the massive Wetterhorn. When you reach Grosse Scheidegg, you have several options. You can continue walking down to **Grindelwald** (2 hours) or take the bus back to **Grindelwald** (35 minutes). The bus runs about every hour.

Another option, if you arrive at Grosse Scheidegg in the early afternoon, is to return to **Interlaken** via the circle route by way of **Meiringen** and **Brienz**. You start this trip with the bus from Grosse Scheidegg over the pass to **Schwarzwaldalp** (15 minutes). Here you change and take the bus to **Meiringen** (45 minutes), then complete your circle trip by taking the train to **Interlaken** (30 minutes). This is a full day trip with some time to explore the village of **Meiringen**. When the train arrives at Brienz (15 minutes), you will see the steamer pulling up to the dock. If you want a steamer adventure, it is an easy seven-minute connection from the train to the steamer, with a short walk to the dock from the train. From here, it is a lovely 1½ hour ride on the **Brienzersee** to Interlaken.

Wetterhorn

OPTION C: To The Faulhorn   Fairly Strenuous 3 Hour Hike

This is one of the outstanding hikes in the Alps. You start at the **First** station (7216 ft) with an easy walk to the Bachalpsee. Then continue on the mountain trail for a fairly strenuous hike to the **Faulhorn** mountain hotel (8794 ft) (☎ 036/53-27-13). Plan to have dinner and spend the night. It is necessary to make a reservation. There are a few private rooms (without bath) and a dormitory. In good weather, you will see a glorious sunrise and the entire panorama of the Bernese Oberland. This is one of the great vistas to behold.

The next morning after breakfast, you can hike back to **First**, or continue on to **Schynige Platte**. It is approximtely a 2½ hour hike back to **First**, where you take the Gondola down to **Grindelwald**. If you continue on to **Schynige Platte** (6488 ft) to the west, it is a 4-5 hour downhill hike. This is a fairly strenuous hike, but a rewarding experience. At Schynige Platte, take the cog train to **Wilderswil** and the train back to Interlaken.

Another option is to take the two-hour hike down from the Faulhorn to **Bussalp** (5996 ft) and the bus down to **Grindelwald**.

You will need lightweight boots for this hike and an overnight pack if you plan to spend the night at the Faulhorn Hotel. The view of the snowcapped mountains to the south and the Brienzersee and green mountains to the north is unsurpassed. The trip to the Faulhorn should only be done in good weather.

If you get an early start, this can be a nice all-day hike from First to Schynige Platte. It takes about 6½ hours walking time. If you want to go from Schynige Platte to First, it is a little more strenuous, but equally rewarding. You will greet many Swiss on the trail.

Sunrise from the Faulhorn

4. THUNERSEE STEAMER

A relaxing steamer ride on the Thunersee with stops at charming, colorful villages.

Round-Trip Time from Interlaken 3-4 Hours (½ day)

No change in Elevation

Walking: Little required, however, Thun is a beautiful walking
       city to explore.

Clear, overcast or rainy day   Information ☎ (033) 36-02-58

Option A: The Niederhorn via Funicular/Chairlift 3-4 Hours

The steamer provides an excellent change of pace and a contrast to the scenery if you have been up in the mountains. Take the steamer from **Interlaken West**. The dock is a short walk from the station. After backing out of the canal, the steamer heads up the lake in the direction of **Thun**.

During the two-hour ride, the steamer makes 11 to 12 stops along the shore to pick up passengers with their bicycles and baby carriages. Many of the docks, where the steamer stops for only a minute or two, display colorful flags and flowers.

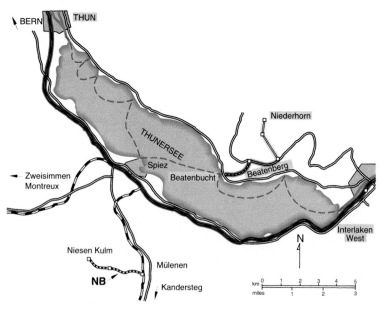

The ride on the Thunersee is most picturesque with magnificient views of the landscape and a pleasant opportunity for lunch. The last stop is **Thun,** a charming medieval town.

There are many beautiful villages, some with medieval castles such as **Thun, Spiez**, **Hilterfingen** and **Oberhofen**. These castles are now museums. There are many fine hotels and restaurants in the villages. Be sure to get a brochure with map from the officer when you board the steamer.

When you arrive at **Thun**, the train station is across the street. You can take the train back to **Interlaken**, which is only 16 miles away and takes less than 30 minutes. Another alternative is to take the time to visit this medieval fortress town. If you walk north on the Bahnhofstrasse to the old town, you will cross the Aare River twice. Just after the second bridge, you will come to Hauptgasse; turn left on this old street with its charming shops. When you arrive at the town square, you can clearly see the great Schloss (castle) which dominates the town. The Castle is now a museum and well worth a visit. After exploring the city, stop for coffee and pastry before returning to the station. Then catch the train to **Interlaken** with a ride along the south shore of the **Thunersee**.

OPTION A: The Niederhorn   **3-4 Hours**

Take the steamer from **Interlaken West** and get off at **Beatenbucht**. This is a ride of just under one hour with several stops along the way. After a two-minute walk to the **Thunersee Beatenberg Bahn (TBB)**, the funicular carries you in ten minutes to the TBB station west of **Beatenberg** (3680 ft). Here you take the bus or a 20-minute walk to the Niederhorn chair lift. This two-section chair lift to the **Niederhorn** (6376 ft) takes 18 minutes, and rewards you with an expansive view of the Thunersee and the mountains.

Castle at Oberhofen on the Thunersee

5. BRIENZER ROTHORN

The highest steam locomotive cog-railway in the Alps with spectacular views of the Bernese Oberland massif to the south and the Brienzersee to the west.

Round-Trip Time from Interlaken 4-5 Hours (½ day)

Highest Elevation: 7,433 feet   Rothorn Kulm
Change in Elevation: 5,577 feet   from Interlaken

Walking: very little required

Best on a clear, sunny day   Information ☎ (036) 51-12-32

Option A: Steamer to Iseltwald   **4-5 Hours**
              Steamer from Interlaken Ost to Iseltwald,
              followed by easy 2 hour walk.

Option B: Steamer to Giessbach   **3-4 Hours**
              Steamer from Interlaken Ost to Giessbach
              and the funicular to the Grand Hotel.

Take the narrow gauge SBB train from **Interlaken Ost** to **Brienz**, a 30-minute ride, traveling along the north shore of the lake. The Brienzer Rothorn station is across the street from the SBB station, so little walking is required. **Brienz** is known for its fine woodworking shops, restaurants and hotels. It is situated at the easterly end of the lake about 10 miles from **Interlaken**.

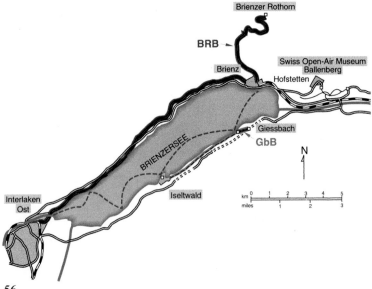

The **Brienzer Rothorn Bahn (BRB)** makes a spectacular climb of 5,560 feet as the train winds its way up the side of the mountain. It takes about one hour to ride one of the seven 90-year-old steam driven trains from **Brienz** (1873 ft) on the lake to the **Rothorn Kulm** (7433 ft). It is a short 15-minute walk to the peak of the Brienzer Rothorn (7708 ft), an ascent of 275 feet.

A hotel, restaurant and sun terrace are at the summit, with magnificent views of the Bernese Oberland to the south. Directly below is the **Brienzersee**, a beautiful wild mountain lake, with steamers plying up and down.

Instead of taking the train to **Brienz**, choose one of the lake steamers leaving every hour from the landing at **Interlaken Ost**, a few steps north of the Interlaken Ost rail station. It takes a little under 1¼ hours for this delightful trip to Brienz. This will add some time to your trip, but well worth it. The landing or dock at **Brienz** is very close to the rail station.

The **Swiss Open Air Museum - Ballenberg** is located 4 miles from Brienz. See Excursion B, page 73, for this all-day activity.

Brienzer Rothorn Bahn (BRB)

OPTION A: Steamer to Iseltwald   4-5 Hours

Take the steamer from the dock at **Interlaken Ost** to **Iseltwald**. This ride on the lake is just under 45 minutes. At the third or fourth stop, depending on the steamer, get off at **Iseltwald**. Walk back one block and turn left (east) and, in a few minutes, you will be walking along the lake towards **Giessbach**. This is an easy two-hour walk, mostly in the shade along the lake.

When you arrive at Giessbach, you can take the steamer on to Brienz, then back to Interlaken, or spend some time at Giessbach as described in Option B.

OPTION B: Steamer to Giessbach   3-4 Hours

Whether you have been up at the **Brienzer Rothorn** or **Interlaken** in the morning, take the steamer to **Giessbach**. From **Brienz**, it is a 10-minute ride; from Interlaken, about one hour. When you arrive at Giessbach, walk several steps to the right from the dock to the **Giessbach Bahn (GbB)**. This funicular takes you up 295 feet in four minutes to the **Grand Hotel Giessbach**. A turn-of-the-century hotel, this is a delightful place to have lunch or tea. From the Terrace, you can see the bridge and the Giessbach Falls cascading in a series of towering waterfalls over the rocks into the lake below. After lunch, take the steamer back to Interlaken, or take the steamer to Brienz and from there catch the train back to Interlaken.

This trip and both options can be done in one day. Catch the morning train to **Brienz**, then the BRB steam train to the Brienzer Rothorn. When you return to the station, take the steamer to **Giessbach** and the funicular up to the Grand Hotel. Returning to the lake, walk west to Iseltwald and catch the steamer to **Interlaken**. Or, if you decide against this two-hour walk, take the steamer back to Interlaken.

Giessbach Falls and the Brienzersee

6. MÄNNLICHEN

**One of the most scenic mountain walks in the Jungfrau region.
Ride the cableway from Wengen to Männlichen and walk down to
Kleine Scheidegg.**

Round-trip Time from Interlaken 4-5 hours (½ day)

Highest Elevation:	7,314 feet	Männlichen Station
Change in Elevation:	5,458 feet	from Interlaken

Walking: Easy 1½ hour downhill walk with a descent of 544 feet.

Best in clear, sunny weather   Information ☎ (036) 55-29-33

Option A: Walk - Kleine Scheidegg to Wengen   2 Hours

Option B: Train - Kleine Scheidegg to Jungfraujoch   3-4 Hours
Walk to Kleine Scheidegg and ride the Jungfrau Bahn up
to the Jungfraujoch. (Trip #1)

This is one of the most beautiful, easy mountain walks in the area. The
walk itself is 2½ miles with a descent of 544 feet from the
Männlichen station (7314 ft) to **Kleine Scheidegg** (6770 ft). It takes
about 1½ hours. If you walk slowly and picnic along the way, allow
some extra time.

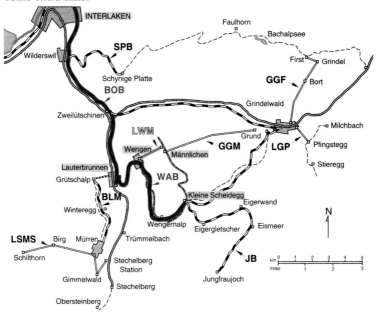

Take the BOB train from **Interlaken Ost** to **Lauterbrunnen**. Change to the WAB line for the cog rail train to **Wengen** (4180 ft). This is a 15-minute trip. From the **Wengen** station, it is a 10-15 minute walk to the **Luftseilbahn Wengen-Männlichen (LWM)** cableway. Walk up the main street and follow the signs for the cableway. You will pass the English Church; the cable car is ahead to the right. The **Wengen-Männlichen (LWM)** cable car to the **Männlichen** station (7314 ft) is a six-minute ride. Travel time from the **Interlaken** station to the station at **Männlichen** is about 1¼ hours.

If you want a moderate climb, turn left as you leave the **Männlichen** station and walk up to the top of **Männlichen** (7685 ft). This is a 371-foot climb. From the top, you have an excellent view looking north to the **Thunersee**, **Interlaken**, **Schynige Platte** and the **Faulhorn**. To the south, there is the noblest of views: from the snowcapped **Wetterhorn** to the **Jungfrau Massif** to the **Schilthorn** with **Tschuggen** (8265 ft) in the foreground.

If you don't want to climb to the top of **Männlichen**, as you exit the cable car, turn right and proceed to the observation point. This is one of the best views of **Wengen** and the Lauterbrunnen valley. Across the valley, you will see the village of **Mürren** (5396 ft), the **Schilthorn** (9744 ft) and the station at **Grütschalp** (4874 ft).

Head south past the restaurant and the **Gondolabahn Grindelwald-Männlichen (GGM)** cableway towards the mountains. There will be the familiar yellow sign pointing the way to **Kleine Scheidegg**. The path will bear to the left, past a small pond. You will be walking into the mountains, most of the time in the sun. A few areas will be in the shade as you walk behind **Tschuggen**.

There are no restaurants until you arrive at **Kleine Scheidegg**, 1½ hours away. You may want to pack a picnic lunch and stop at one

Cable Car above Wengen (LWM)

Kleine-Scheidegg beneath the Junfrau

of the benches along the way to feast and enjoy the splendor of the mountains in front of you. **Grindelwald** will be in the Alpine basin below and, to the south, the massive snowcapped mountains of the **Jungfrau Massif**.

If you start early in the morning, you can plan to have lunch at one of the restaurants in **Kleine Scheidegg**, then take the train back either via **Grindelwald** or **Wengen** and **Lauterbrunnen**. We recommend walking shoes, but you can do the walk in street shoes.

OPTION A - Walk - Kleine Scheidegg to Wengen   2 Hours

For those who would like to continue walking after arriving at **Kleine Scheidegg**, there is a very scenic walk down to **Wengen** past **Wengernalp** (6143 ft). To start this walk, cross the JB tracks at **Kleine Scheidegg** and follow the path to the right. The first part of the trail takes you to **Wengernalp**, approximately 35 minutes. The path then continues down to **Wengen**, approximately 2 hours. At **Wengen**, you can catch the train back to **Lauterbrunnen**. Many people take this beautiful downhill walk with a descent of 2,590 feet. It is well marked and a good path to **Wengen**. Walking shoes or hiking boots necessary.

OPTION B - Train - Kleine Scheidegg to Jungfraujoch   3-4 Hours

If you complete the walk to **Kleine Scheidegg** early and it is a nice clear day, continue the trip up to the **Jungfraujoch**. If you have limited time in the area, it is easy to combine these two trips. Allow 3-4 hours round-trip from **Kleine Scheidegg** to the **Jungfraujoch**. It is expensive, but well worth it.

7. OESCHINENSEE

A most spectacular clear, blue Alpine mountain lake located in the Kandersteg area.

Round-Trip Time from Interlaken 4-5 hours (½ day)		
Highest Elevation:	5,510 feet	Oeschinensee
Change in Elevation:	3,654 feet	from Interlaken
Walking: A 10-minute walk from the station to the chairlift, then a 7-minute ride and an easy 30-minute downhill walk to the Lake with a descent of 285 feet.		
Best in clear, sunny weather	Information	☎(033) 75-11-18

The **Oeschinensee** is, without a doubt, one of the most magnificent mountain lakes in Switzerland. It lies at the foot of the Blümlisalp, which soars overhead to 12,000 feet. In the late afternoon, the mountains reflect off this deep blue, glacier lake.

The lake is off the beaten path but, because of its beauty, many walkers are attracted to the area. For this trip, take the train from **Interlaken** to **Spiez**, then change to the fast train to **Kandersteg** which runs every hour. Total travel time is about one hour. From the Kandersteg station (3856 ft), it is a 10-minute walk to the chairlift.

Take the chairlift, and in seven minutes you will be at 5510 feet. From here, you have an easy 30-minute downhill walk through the meadows and forest to the Oeschinensee (5225 ft). It is a good, wide path, and you will descend 285 feet. You cannot walk around the lake because the mountains form a backdrop with their snowcapped peaks at the top.

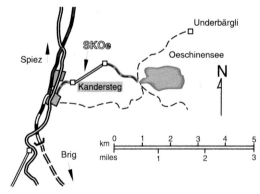

Oeschinensee

There are several hotels and restaurants on the west side of the lake. On the north side, you can see the trail leading up to the SAC Blümlisalp hut (9305 ft). On a clear day, the hut is visible with the Swiss flag flying. This is one of the most difficult climbs and should not be attempted without previous climbing experience. The first stage of the climb to **Underbärgli** (5796 ft) is an ascent of 571 feet from the lake and a little over one mile. It takes about 1½ hours to climb up the ledge on the north side of the lake to Underbärgli. Along the way, you have a splendid view of the Oeschinensee and the mountains to the south. It is a very worthwhile hike up just halfway, about a 45 minute climb.

On the southwesterly end of the Oeschinensee, you can see the trail that leads up to the SAC Frunden hut (8403 ft). This, again, should not be attempted without previous experience. The early part of the climb to the south of the lake is beautiful and well worth doing.

Returning, you have two choices: the 30-minute walk back to the chairlift and down to **Kandersteg**; or the 1½ hour walk down through the forest and pasture on your way back to **Kandersteg**.

This is an easy, relaxing half-day trip to the lake. If you have the extra time, plan to have lunch at the hotel or a picnic along the lake. Explore the shore or try your hand at trout fishing.

Kandersteg and the Oeschinensee are popular for the walks, hikes and climbing. There is a mountaineering school in Kandersteg that teaches children and adults the techniques of climbing.

8. PFINGSTEGG

A cable car ride and a short walk to Stieregg for a splendid view of the Lower Glacier above Grindelwald.

Round-Trip Time from Interlaken 4-5 Hours (½ day)		
Highest Elevation:	5,583 feet	Stieregg
Change in Elevation:	3,727 feet	from Interlaken
Walking: 3 hour walk round-trip with a climb of 1,021 feet		
Best in clear, sunny weather	Information ☎ (036) 53-26-26	

From **Interlaken Ost**, take the BOB train to **Grindelwald** (3390 ft), a 40-minute run. Walk east through the village of Grindelwald. This is a slightly uphill walk. The **First** Gondola station is on your left. Continue another block to the sign for the **Pfingstegg Bahn**. Turn right and walk down the road to the **Luftseilbahn Grindelwald-Pfingstegg (LGP)** cableway. The cable car ascends 1,181 feet in 4 minutes to **Pfingstegg** (4562 ft). At the Pfingstegg station, there is a restaurant and sun terrace. As you leave the station, turn right and follow the path to the Lower Glacier. You will be walking around the Mättenberg, with a superb view of Grindelwald to your right and the rocky east face of the Eiger in front of you. The path over which you will be walking is the accumulated earth and stone deposits carried down hundreds of years ago by the glacier.

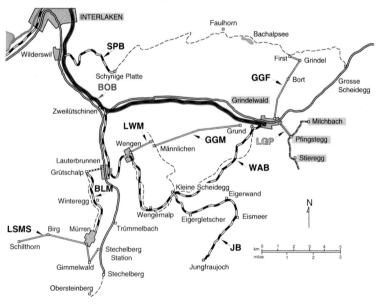

After a 1½ hour climb along the Mättenberg, during which you will round several cliffs, you will arrive at **Stieregg** (5583 ft). This is a beautiful setting with restaurant, sun terrace and a panoramic view of the icy expanse of the Lower Glacier, the Eismeer and the austere flank of the Fiescherhorn. This glacier descends towards Grindelwald between the Mättenberg and the Eiger. For experienced mountaineers only, the path continues to the SAC Schreckhorn hut (8295 ft).

It is an easy downhill walk back to the Pfingstegg station and the cable car to Grindelwald. Or continue hiking down the trail and in about 30 minutes, you will pass the area of **Breitlouwina** which is rich in sediments deposited millions of years ago in the forming of the Mättenberg mountain. In another 30 minutes, you will arrive at **Milchbach** with its restaurant which overlooks the Upper Glacier. From here it is a short walk to the Ice Caves which will take you directly onto the glacier.

This glacier descends towards Grindelwald between the Wetterhorn and the Mättenberg. From the Milchbach, it is a 1½ hour hike down to the Hotel Wetterhorn. At this point, you can return to Grindelwald by bus or continue on with an easy 1½ hour walk.

There are several additional walks in this area. As an example, on your return from Stieregg, you may elect to walk down to the Gletscherschlucht, the glacier gorge which is 15 minutes beyond the old marble quarries.

Stieregg above Grindelwald

9. SCHYNIGE PLATTE

Cog Railway to Schynige Platte and the Alpine Garden with superb views of the snowcapped mountains to the south and the lakes to the north.

Round-Trip Time from Interlaken 4 Hours (½ day)		
Highest Elevation:	6,488 feet	Schynige Platte
Change in Elevation:	4,632 feet	from Interlaken
Walking: very little required		
Best on a clear day	Information	☎ (036) 22-85-44

Take the BOB train from **Interlaken Ost** to **Wilderswil** (1916 ft), a five-minute run. At **Wilderswil**, you will see the little red **Schynige Platte Bahn (SPB)** train across the tracks. A small electric engine pushes the two-car cog train up the winding track to the summit. This line first opened in June 1893 and became part of the BOB system in 1895. It was converted to electric in 1914.

It takes the train almost an hour to climb the 4,572 feet from **Wilderswil** to the station at **Schynige Platte** (6488 ft). It is a very scenic ride, first through the forest and then on to the north side of the mountain. You can see Interlaken and the Thunersee to the west and the Brienzersee to the east. About two-thirds of the way up, the

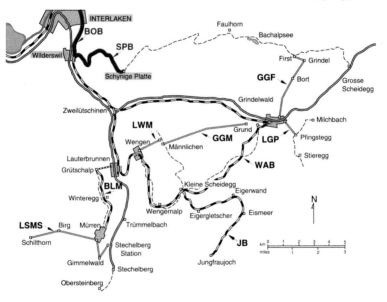

train will make a short stop at **Breitlauenen** (5058 ft) for those who want to do some walking. In just under 20 minutes, the train will twist up to the Schynige Platte station.

At the summit, you will have a broad vista of the snowcapped mountains to the south. Only Männlichen appears to stand between you and the snow-covered north face of the Eiger, the Mönch and the Jungfrau. This is one of the few places where you can travel by cog train and appreciate the full magnitude of the mountains and lakes.

A few steps from the station, you will find a restaurant and an Alpine botanical garden. There are over 500 varieties of plants. Because you are at an altitude close to 7,000 feet, spring does not arrive until early July, when the snow has melted and the sun is warm. Also, there is a circular panoramic walk **(Panoramaweg)** that offers a superb view of the mountains; well worth doing.

Schynige Platte is one of the best vistas, accessible by mountain train, for viewing the mountains, lakes, forests and flowers. It is ideal for children.

Mountain train (SPB) with view of the Thunersee

10. NIESEN

One of the longest funiculars with an exquisite panoramic view of the Alps to the south, the Thunersee to the north, the Brienzersee and Interlaken to the east.

Round-Trip Time from Interlaken 4 hours (½ day)

Highest Elevation:	7,747 feet	Niesen Kulm
Change in Elevation:	5,891 feet	from Interlaken

Walking: very little required

Best in clear, sunny weather   Information ☎(033) 71-11-12

The **Niesen** provides one of the most impressive views of the area, covering the lakes, valleys, forests and snowcapped mountains, including the peaks of the Jungfrau Massif and the Valais Alps to the south. It is an excellent half-day outing.

From **Interlaken**, take the train to **Spiez**. Change to the local train to **Frutigen** and points beyond. Exit at the second stop, **Mülenen** (2270 ft), about seven minutes. Travel time from **Interlaken** is about 45 minutes.

It is a two-minute walk to the **Niesen Bahn (NB)** funicular. This is a two-section funicular to the Niesen Kulm. The first section, a 60 passenger car, takes you to **Schwandegg** (5465 ft). This is a 14-minute

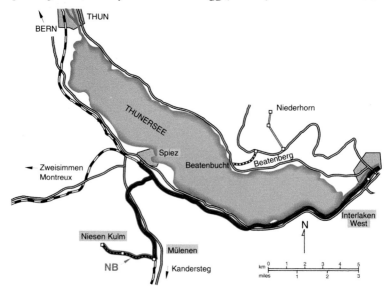

ride up the side of the mountain. You then change to the second section of the funicular which climbs up the sheer side of the mountain to the top station in 12 minutes. This is a spectacular ride during which you will ascend a total of 5,477 feet to the top of the Niesen at 7,747 feet.

The funicular took four years to build and began operating in 1910. There has been a mountain hotel at the top of the Niesen since 1856. Supplies were brought up by mule trains in the early days.

It is an amazing journey with a maximum gradient of 68%. At the top, there is the **Hotel Niesenkulm** with restaurant. This is a lovely summit panorama of the Alps with a bird's-eye view of the **Thunersee**, **Interlaken** and the **Brienzersee**.

For those in good condition, the walk down from the Niesen Kulm takes a little over 3 hours. From the intermediate station at Schwandegg, there are a number of interesting walking routes.

The Niesen is very easily recognized by its distinctive pyramid shape that juts high in the sky behind Spiez.

Niesen viewed from the Thunersee

EXCURSIONS

A. GEMMI PASS
B. SWISS OPEN AIR MUSEUM - BALLENBERG
C. BERN
D. LUZERN

We recommend four exceptional all-day excursions: Hike across the Bernese Oberland, Historical Museum, The Capital of Switzerland, and Europe's famous Covered Bridge. Each one is unique.

A. GEMMI PASS　　　**All-Day Trip**

A combination of trains, bus and cableway up the Valais to Brig and Leukerbad, including a 3½ hour downhill walk north across the Bernese Oberland to Kandersteg.　　Information　☎ (027) 61-18-39

On a clear day, take an early morning train from **Interlaken West** to **Spiez** (30 minutes), then change to the fast train to **Brig** (65 minutes). You will travel through the nine-mile long Lötschberg rail tunnel between **Kandersteg** and the Valais, with a long descent to **Brig**. At **Brig**, change to the Sion and Lausanne train, getting off at **Lenk**. If you take the local, get off at the fifth stop (25 minutes.) If you are on the fast train, **Lenk** is the second stop (20 minutes.)

From the Lenk station, take the bus to **Leukerbad**. This is a wild 10-mile bus ride and takes about 35 minutes. **Leukerbad** (4671 ft) is a health resort well-known for its mineral baths and good food.

So far, you have been on three trains and a bus. Elapsed time to **Leukerbad** is about 3 hours. Don't give up; the best is yet to come.

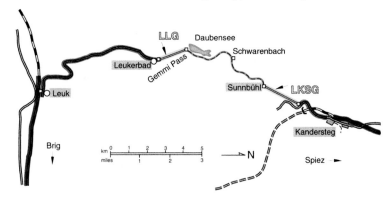

From the bus stop, you walk north through town to the **Luftseilbahn Leukerbad-Gemmipass (LLG)**, a 15-minute walk. You will see the cableway as you approach the sheer mountain cliff. At the LLG station, take the cable car to the **Gemmi Pass** (7616 ft). This is an ascent of 2,945 feet. The cable car is a five-minute ride compared to a very strenuous 2-3 hour climb.

At the top, you will find the Hotel Wildstrubel with restaurant and sun terrace. You are overlooking the Rhône Valley and the mountains to the south - the Matterhorn and Weisshorn, a great panorama of snowcapped mountains and a pleasant stop for lunch.

You may choose, however, to be on your way to **Kandersteg**. When you leave the Gemmi cable car, walk down to the **Daubensee** and follow the trail on the east side of the lake. The lake is almost one mile long. If you brought a picnic lunch, a perfect stop would be along the east shore of the **Daubensee**. The walk to **Sunnbühl** (6359 ft) and the cable car will be about 3½ hours. It is an easy 1,257-foot downhill descent along the five-mile walk.

About halfway (1½ hours walking), you will see the formidable **Schwarenbach Mountain Hotel** (6780 ft). This was originally the Customs House between the old Switzerland and the Valais. This is a good opportunity to freshen up and have lunch. After you leave the hotel, you will note a change in the terrain, as you pass several bends in the trail and descend onto a plateau. A little further on, the path will curve to the left and you will see the **Luftseilbahn Kandersteg Sunnbühl-Gemmi (LKSG)** cableway.

The cable car takes you down in 25 minutes into the Kander valley, just south of **Kandersteg**. Generally, there is a bus waiting to take you to the Kandersteg station 10 minutes away, where you catch the train back to **Interlaken**, about a 1¼ hour trip with a change at **Spiez**.

Daubensee - Gemmi Walk

B. SWISS OPEN AIR MUSEUM

C. BERN

D. LUZERN

B. SWISS OPEN AIR MUSEUM - BALLENBERG

This museum of Swiss rural dwellings and life-styles has over 60 historical buildings with almost every canton represented. It is situated on 125 acres in a parklike setting outside of Brienz. A variety of rural crafts are demonstrated in and around the farmhouses and ancillary buildings utilizing the earlier tools and techniques. The Museum farmers cultivate the fields using the old traditional methods. It presents a comprehensive picture of life as it existed in rural Switzerland many years ago. This museum is definitely worth a visit.

*Take the train or steamer from **Interlaken Ost** to **Brienz**, then catch the bus to the West entrance at Hofstetten, an 8 minute ride (4 miles). For information* ☎ *(036) 51-11-23.*

C. BERN - CAPITAL OF SWITZERLAND

Bern is a unique and charming city. It is the capital of Switzerland and the capital of the canton of Bern. Its romantic, medieval streets with over four miles of arcades are the longest covered shopping promenade in the world. It is a perfect strolling town with hundreds of shops and popular cafes, ideal for a rainy day visit. The city is the fourth largest in Switzerland and filled with museums, theatres, churches, fountains, Bear Pits and the world famous Clock Tower. This is an exciting city to visit

*Take the train from **Interlaken** to **Bern**, a delightful 55-minute ride along the south shore of the Thunersee. Visit the Tourist Office in the Bern rail station for maps and brochures.*

D. LUZERN

Luzern is one of the most popular and often visited cities in Switzerland. It is well known for the covered wooden Chapel Bridge (Kapellbrüche) built in 1333. The Bridge is a grand representation of the art of medieval architecture with its numerous gable paintings and large octagonal water tower. Visit the old town across the river with the many frescoed houses and the famous Swiss Transport Museum. Luzern is a great city for walking, sightseeing and shopping.

*Take the fast train from **Interlaken Ost** to **Luzern**. The train follows the north shore of the lake to Brienz and to Meiringen. After changing direction, the train continues over the Brünig Pass and arrives in Luzern in just under two hours.*

BERNESE OBERLAND - Towns & Villages

INTERLAKEN (1856 ft) is the central point of the Bernese Oberland. It has a population of 5,200 and sits on the Bödeli, a two-mile flat section of land between the Thunersee and the Brienzersee. All the roads and trains in the area lead to Interlaken. This is an old town, dating back to the 12th century, that grew up around the Augustinian Convent. The convent was dissolved in 1528. During the 1800's, the village grew and the first steamers appeared on the Thunersee and the Brienzersee. By 1890, mountain trains were running between Interlaken and Grindelwald and Lauterbrunnen. In 1891, the town name was changed from Aarmüle to Interlaken.

Today, Interlaken is a thriving and active center. The Höheweg is the main avenue with many fine hotels, restaurants, shops, and borders the Höhematte, the largest park in town.

Interlaken has two train stations. **Interlaken West**, in the central part of town, is the main station, located adjacent to the steamer landing for the Thunersee. The **Interlaken Ost** (East) station is about 2 miles to the east on the Höheweg. The Interlaken Ost station is the termination point for all the trains. The main line of the Swiss Federal Railway (SBB) feeds in from Bern and Spiez. The narrow gauge SBB line feeds from Luzern and Brienz. The Bernese Oberland Bahn (BOB) originates here and goes up the valley to Grindelwald and Lauterbrunnen. Just a few steps north of the Interlaken Ost station is the very convenient landing for the steamers on the Brienzersee. The PTT buses stop at both stations and travel to the outlying villages and around the Thunersee.

MOUNTAIN VILLAGES

There are many charming villages in the mountains and surrounding the lakes. The four mountain villages, **Grindelwald**, **Wengen**, **Mürren** and **Kandersteg**, are the best known.

Grindelwald and the Wetterhorn

GRINDELWALD (3390 ft) is a charming village of 3,500 people situated in a lush basin surrounded by the snowcapped peaks of the Eiger, Schreckhorn and the Wetterhorn to the south. It is one of the most popular summer and winter resorts. The Grindelwald Glaciers are formed between the mountains and flow into the Schwarze Lütschine River, which rushes south of town along the valley towards the Brienzersee. The massive Eiger is a short distance to the south and the Wetterhorn to the East. Grindelwald is accessible by car and the BOB mountain train. It is a bustling tourist center with many tour buses.

WENGEN (4180 ft) is a cheerful mountain village of 1,200 people and overlooks the Lauterbrunnen Valley and the Weisse Lütschine River. It is situated on a plateau high above the valley. The Jungfrau, with its perpetual snowcover, looms in front of the village only 5 miles to the south. Wengen is a quiet, sunny and car-free village, accessible only by mountain train or walking. This is a summer and winter resort with many sophisticated shops. The English are quite fond of Wengen. The sunsets, with the alpine glow, are most spectacular from Wengen.

Wengen and the Junfrau

Approximately the last weekend of September, Wengen is a wonderful place to be when the cows come down from the summer pastures on their way to the Lauterbrunnen valley below. Their heads are "dressed" in flowers and their bells ring out as they make the journey down the mountain and parade through the town.

MÜRREN (5396 ft) is a sheltered traffic-free resort on a ledge overlooking the Lauterbrunnen valley from the west. From Mürren, Wengen is visible to the north, on the opposite side of the valley, with the massive Schwarzmönch and the Jungfrau to the east. Mürren is

Mürren - Dorfstrasse with the Eiger

76

the highest village in the Bernese Oberland and somewhat remote. It has a population of 500 people and is accessible by cable car and train. It has an easy going charm about it and is definitely influenced by its proximity to the mountains.

KANDERSTEG (3856 ft) is a picturesque mountain village of 1,100 people situated at the head of the Kandertal Valley. The nine-mile long Lötschberg rail tunnel begins at Kandersteg and crosses over to Brig in the Valais. Most people drive here for the rail transport of their cars through the tunnel to Brig. Others come here to walk and hike. This unspoiled mountaineering resort, surrounded by snowcapped peaks, is away from the main tourist route. You won't find many tour buses. One of the outstanding features is the cobalt blue Oeschinensee at the foot of the Blümlisalphorn, Frundenhorn and the Doldenhorn. It is one of the most beautiful lakes in the Bernese Oberland.

Kandersteg and BLS Railway Car Loading for Lötschberg Tunnel

There are many other charming villages in the mountains and valleys around the lakes. If you only have a few days and this is your first trip, we suggest you stay in one of the four mountain villages or in Interlaken. Explore from there.

FOOD & DRINK IN THE BERNESE OBERLAND

The food in the Bernese Oberland is excellent. It ranges from the best international cuisine to a slice of pizza, and from the regional Swiss dishes to specialty game dinners in the fall.

There is more to the area than mountains, valleys and lakes. Experience the many different regional dishes and pastries, the local cheeses and the wide selection of wines and beers.

Most of the hotels and restaurants have people who speak English, and they can assist you with the many different dishes. Often there is an English menu.

Restaurants - The Swiss pride themselves on serving good food. The larger hotels serve elegant continental or French dishes, and the smaller hotels and restaurants serve the regional food which is in the German style - large portions of meat and potatoes or pasta. You will eat well in any restaurant - hotel, mountain, steamer or train. Tips are automatically included in the bill. Request an up-to-date list of restaurants from your hotel or tourist office.

The local food and drink should be part of your experience in Switzerland - savor it to the fullest.

Breakfast - Frühstück

Your day will begin with **breakfast (Frühstück)**, generally served until 10:00 a.m. Usually included in the price of the hotel room, it is a Continental breakfast consisting of rich coffee and hot chocolate with a large selection of wonderful breads, rolls and croissants. Slice off a piece of the different breads, add from the selection of jams (be sure to try the Black Cherry jam) or honey. Enjoy the variety of meats, such as ham, veal sausage or salami, with one of the many cheeses. Most places also offer cereals, yogurt and Muesli. Eat a hearty breakfast and be off on your trip for the day.

Lunch - Mittagessen

In the villages, most shops, banks and tourist offices close for **lunch** (**Mittagessen**) from noon until 1:30 or 2:00 p.m. Some people make this their main meal of the day. Many of the mountain restaurants are self-service and feature a **Tagesteller** or special plate of the day. This generally is a serving of meat, potatoes and vegetables. After a morning walk, such a meal is very satisfying. Or select a salad such as **Grüner Salat** (a mixed green salad) or **Gemischter Salat** (salad with vegetables) topped with French or Italian dressing.

Other popular luncheon items include a rich assortment of sausages, such as **Bratwurst** with **Zwiebel** (onion) sauce and **Rösti** (hash brown potatoes.) Or the **Schnitzel** (pork or veal) with **Pommes Frites** (french fried potatoes) and a salad. The soups are tasty; try the **Gulaschsuppe** (goulash soup), a thick meat and vegetable soup with a roll. It is a very hearty meal. A full selection of bottled water, soft drinks, wines and beers is available.

Another possibility for lunch is to create your own "picnic" to enjoy on a bench on one of the mountain trails or by the lake. Start with the "Bäckerei" (bakery) for fresh rolls. Then head to the "Metzgerei" (butcher shop) for ham, salami, wurst or **"Bünderfleisch"** (the thin sliced air dried beef from Graubünden). You may want to try some of the local cheeses or triangles of Gruyére cheese, along with a piece of fruit. Don't forget to take along a **Toblerone** chocolate bar. In some of the markets, you can purchase everything at one time, including a bottle of wine or water.

If you are going to be on one of the lake steamers, consider having lunch on board. They have a great selection of meals from sandwiches and salads to a full luncheon.

In the afternoon, don't miss the **Konditorei** or Tea Room. This is an opportunity to try the many different Swiss pastries, such as **Apfelkuchen** (apple pastry) or **Obsttorten** (fruit tarts such as peach, strawberry or plum). The chocolate cakes are delicious, as is the ice cream sundae (Coupe Denmark). Another popular Swiss dessert is **Vermicelli**, a chestnut-flavored mousse.

Dinner - Abendessen

Dinner is generally served beginning at 6:30 p.m. You have a wide selection from the hotel dining rooms to the many restaurants in the towns or villages. Most meals start with soup, then the main course and a salad. Many restaurants now offer a selection of portion sizes to accommodate the new eating habits of lighter food and smaller portions:

> The **full course** is a large meal and frequently includes a second serving from the hot plate.

> The **plate** is a smaller portion with everything served on the plate at one time - no second servings.

> The **mini portion** is for the light eater or for the person who wants to try several mini portions of different dishes.

If you are fortunate enough to be in the Bernese Oberland during September and October, you can feast on a **"Wild Game"** dinner, generally a roast saddle of **Rehrücken** (Venison) or **Chamois** (mountain goat) with Rösti potatoes or Spätzli, red cabbage, chanterelle mushrooms, cranberry compote and chestnuts. This is a real treat.

****

Below is a list of Swiss specialty foods to look for:

> **Cheese Fondue** began as a cheese soup and is now a meal. A typical fondue consists of three different cheeses cooked with white wine over a flame. Chunks of crusty white bread are dipped into the melted cheese mixture.

> **Bölledünne** - Onion Pie served hot with a glass of white wine.

> **Fondue Bourguignonne** - a beef fondue with various vegetables, fruits and sauces. The **Chinoise** version is prepared with hot broth in place of the oil.

> **Raclette** - a specialty from the Valais, heated cheese is scraped onto a plate and served with boiled potatoes and pearl onions.

> **Kalbsbraten** - a delicious Roast Veal

Bratwurst - The staple sausage served with a roll or, as an entree, with an onion sauce and Rösti potatoes.

Bündnerfleisch - Thinly sliced air dried beef from Graubünden. Great as an appetizer or for lunch and especially good for a hike.

Landjäger - A smoked sausage that keeps well unrefrigerated. Good choice for a hike.

Berner Platte - Generous portions of ham and sausage served with sauerkraut and potatoes. A hearty meal.

Rösti - Swiss hash brown potatoes

Spätzli - A dumpling-style pasta

Geschnetzeltes Kalbfleisch - Sautéed strips of veal in a mushroom cream sauce served with Rösti potatoes. This is an excellent Zürich dish on most menus.

Eglifilets in Weisswein - Filets of Perch in white wine sauce with mushrooms.

Schnitzel - Fried filet of veal or pork. This is the most popular meat dish in the country.

Rahmschnitzel - Veal or Pork filets sautéed in wine and butter and topped with a special cream sauce.

The Swiss are known for their soups. All are good and hearty. Try the **Erbsensuppe**, a thick pea soup; **Gemüsesuppe**, a vegetable soup; or you might try the soup of the day, **Tagessuppe**.

Fish

The many wonderful lakes in Switzerland produce a wide variety of fresh fish. The Brienzersee and Thunersee produce several delicious species such as: **Forellen** (Trout), **Hecht** (Pike), **Felchen** (Fera), **Egli** (Perch).

Cheese

The two most famous cheeses in Switzerland are the Emmentaler and Gruyère. They are often used in fondue. **Emmentaler**, the Swiss cheese with the holes, is semihard with a nutlike flavor. **Gruyère** is a firmer cheese with smaller holes and a nutty flavor.

In the Bernese Oberland, the cows graze in the high Alps during the summer, and the herdsmen make cheese with the milk produced at the higher elevations. Most villages have a cheese shop and sell the mountain and valley cheeses, little of which is exported or shipped out of the area. Visit the village cheese shop and taste the different cheeses: **Alpkäse, Sefener Saustaler, Wengen-Mutschli, Justistal Käse, Brienzer-Mutschli**, and the goat cheeses such as **Ziegenkäse, Spätener, Breitlauener**.

Wines

The Swiss wines are light, fruity, fragrant and delicious. Very little of the Swiss wine is exported, so this is a good opportunity to enjoy the local wines. In the restaurants, you can either select a bottle of wine or the **Offene Wein** (open wine) served in a carafe. Some of the popular Swiss "open wines" are **Dôle** and **Salvagnin** (Reds) and **Fendant** and **Féchy** (Whites).

The most popular bottled Swiss red wine is the **Dôle** from the Valais. The most popular bottled white wine is the **Fendant**, also from the Valais. In addition, the Swiss produce excellent **Merlot** and **Pinot Noir** red wines. Several excellent white wines include the **Féchy**, **Dézaley, Aigle, Epesses, Yvorne** and **St. Saphorin**.

Spirits

The most popular Swiss fruit brandy is the **Poire Williams** made from pears in the Valais. Drink it "neat" and cold. Other popular and excellent fruit brandies are **Kirsch** made from cherries and **Pflümli** made from plums.

Beer

If you like beer, you will enjoy the Swiss beer. The leading brands are **Feldschlösschen** from Rheinfelden and **Cardinal** from Fribourg. Look for **Rugenbräu**, a local beer brewed in Interlaken.

Chocolate

The Swiss are famous for their chocolate - milk or bittersweet, chocolate mousse, chocolate and thick cream, or a chocolate sundae "Coupe Denmark". Put a chocolate bar in your day pack to eat on one of your walks.

SUMMER SPORTS

A full range of sporting activities is available in the area. Most of the towns and villages have **tennis courts, swimming pools** and **miniature golf.**

Contact the tourist office in the town in which you are staying to make the necessary arrangements.

MOUNTAINEERING

Mountaineering was pioneered by the British and Swiss during the last half of the 1800's. The **Swiss Alpine Club (SAC)** was founded in 1863. The SAC operates over 160 mountain huts throughout the Alps with a network of trails for easy access.

If you want to try mountain climbing, rock climbing and rappeling, start with one of the mountaineering schools in **Grindelwald, Kandersteg** or **Meiringen.** A first ascent can be made on your initial trip. Mountain Guides are also available in **Wengen** and **Mürren.**

It is best to meet your English-speaking guide the day or night before to be sure you understand what to expect on the trip the next day. Children from ages seven and older will find that mountaineering is one of the highlights of their trip to the Alps.

It is important that you be in excellent physical shape if you plan to do a serious climb, and only climb with a guide who has the necessary equipment. You will need to make arrangements in advance.

Contact the **Mountaineering Schools**:

> CH-3718 Kandersteg, Switzerland
> Telephone: (033) 75 13 52 or 75 17 48
>
> CH-3818 Grindelwald, Switzerland
> Telephone: (036) 53 52 00
>
> CH-3860 Meiringen, Switzerland
> Telephone: (036) 71 35 37 or 71 47 26

Contact the Tourist Offices in Kandersteg, Grindelwald, Wengen or Mürren by telephone or FAX before you leave home.

GOLF

There is an excellent golf course two miles west of Interlaken in Unterseen. This is an 18 hole, par 72 course. Overall length of the course is 6,680 yards. A club house, restaurant and pro shop are open to the public. Call ahead for reservations.

> Interlaken-Unterseen Golf Course
> Telephone: (036) 22 60 22
> FAX: (036) 22 76 79
>
> *Open April 1 to October 31*

Additional sports activities in the area include:

> Paragliding
> Mountain Biking
> Horseback Riding
> Sailing
> Wind Surfing
> Fishing

Arrangements can be made through the local tourist office.

Tourist Offices	
3800 **Interlaken**	Tel: (036) 22 21 21
	FAX: (036) 22 52 21
3818 **Grindelwald**	Tel: (036) 53 12 12
	FAX: (036) 53 30 80
3823 **Wengen**	Tel: (036) 55 14 14
	FAX: (036) 55 30 60
3825 **Mürren**	Tel: (036) 55 16 16
	FAX: (036) 55 37 69
3718 **Kandersteg**	Tel: (033) 75 12 34
	FAX: (033) 75 16 10

CASTLES IN THE BERNESE OBERLAND

There are many castles in Switzerland, many of which now house excellent museums. The four castles listed here are all within 16 miles of Interlaken.

Oberhofen Castle
CH 3653 Oberhofen
Telephone: (033) 43-12-35
Mid-May to mid-October - Closed Monday Mornings

This castle dates back to the 12th century. Today, the castle combines seven centuries of modification. Under the auspices of the Bernese Historical Museum, the rooms of the castle have been transformed into a museum, which depicts the Bernese nobility style of living from the Middle Ages to the time of Napoleon III.

Hünegg Castle
CH 3652 Hilterfingen
Telephone: (033) 43-19-82
Mid-May to mid-October

Hünegg Castle was built in the 19th century in a setting typical of the French Renaissance Period. In 1966, the castle was opened as the Museum of History, with the existing furnishings in place from the 19th century. A collection of the works of the Bernese painter, Martin Lauterburg (1891-1960) is housed in the Castle.

Thun Castle
CH 3600 Thun
Telephone: (033) 23-20-01
April to September

Thun Castle with its huge tower constructed at the end of the 12th century is a prominent landmark. The Historical Museum was founded in 1888. The focal point of the museum is the Knights' Hall with the original fireplace. The exhibition includes an extensive collection of furniture and toys and a display of the Federal Defense Department.

Spiez Castle
CH 3700 Spiez
Telephone: (033) 54-15-06
Good Friday to mid-October Closed Monday mornings

The Spiez Castle origins began with the Tower which dates back to the 12th century. Other buildings belonging to the castle complex actually predate the castle, such as an early Norman church built approximately in the year 1000. The Spiez Castle is very much alive during the season with special exhibitions in the museum, concerts and open-air performances.

****

All castles can be reached by lake steamer on the Thunersee, bus or car. The castles at Thun and Spiez can also be reached by train.

SWISS TRANSPORTATION

The core of the Swiss public transportation is the **Swiss Federal Railways (SBB)**. This agency operates the rail network of over 3,100 miles of public and private rail companies. It is the best in the world. Additional areas of public transportation include the lake steamers, buses, funiculars, cableways and city transportation systems. The coordination between the various transportation enterprises is called the **Swiss Travel System (STS)** and benefits the public with excellent and efficient services. The concept of the Swiss rail system is to have **"a train every hour on every line**."

More people depend on public transportation in Switzerland than in any other European country. It is efficient, clean and on time. In addition to transporting people, the rail system offers a distinct advantage in the transportation of luggage. The SBB trains feed into the **Zürich** and **Geneva** airports so when you arrive, for a small fee, you can check your bags through to the railway station in the town or village in which you will be staying. This service is called the **"Fly-Rail Baggage."** This permits you to take advantage of the region through which you are traveling unencumbered by your luggage. As an example, you may elect to go part way by train, then steamer or bus, without the concern of handling your luggage, which will be at your destination, generally before you arrive.

The following is a description of the four Swiss Travel System Passes and Cards that can be purchased to make your travel as easy as possible:

The **Swiss Pass** allows non-residents great flexibility in using the public transportation network throughout the country on an unlimited basis for 8 days, 15 days or one month. The **Swiss Pass** must be purchased outside of Switzerland. The **Swiss Pass** will take you within the Bernese Oberland on the mountain trains as far as **Grindelwald, Wengen** and **Mürren**. Travel beyond these villages up into the mountains qualifies for a 25% fare reduction. The **Swiss Pass** is a great value for traveling in Switzerland on the 9,000-mile network of trains, postal buses, steamers and local street cars and bus service in the 30 major cities.

The **Swiss Flexi Pass** is valid for travel any 3 days within a 15-day period. It has the same benefits as a Swiss Pass, except for a shorter period. This is for non-residents and must be purchased outside of Switzerland.

The **Swiss Card** is valid for one month. It includes one free transfer within Switzerland to your destination to be completed within one day of arrival, and one free transfer to airport or border to be completed within one day of departure. Plus, you receive a 50% discount on all tickets for the public transportation system, as well as most mountain trains, funiculars and cableways. This is for non-residents and must be purchased outside of Switzerland.

The **Bernese Oberland Regional Pass** can be purchased in Switzerland. It is valid for 15 days, including 5 days of unlimited travel and 10 days at half-fare on specified routes, with 25% off on the mountaintop trains and cableways. The Regional Pass is valid from May through October.

The **Eurailpass** is valid in Switzerland except on the mountain trains, cableways and funiculars. You can travel as far as **Interlaken** by train or steamer on a Eurailpass. A separate ticket is required to ride the mountain trains.

If you arrive by Eurailpass or by car and plan to visit for 4 or 5 days, we suggest you get a **Bernese Oberland Regional Pass**. This will permit you to enjoy the mountain trains, funiculars, cableways and steamers without the need to purchase tickets for each trip. The Jungfrau and Schilthorn are expensive trips, even with your 25% discount, but very worthwhile on a clear day. (see Map Page 17)

A few notes on transportation:

- Children under 16 years travel free with at least one
  adult. There is no discount for Senior citizens.

- The official Swiss timetable is printed each June and
  is valid for one year.

- For the most part, the timetable is the same for all days
  of the week and holidays.

- Baggage can be checked from one train station to another
  train station for a small fee. Take advantage of this
  service.

- **Wengen** and **Mürren** do not permit automobiles. If you are driving, you will need to park your car in the Park Haus (garage) in Lauterbrunnen which is adjacent to the rail station. **Wengen** can be reached by train in 14 minutes and **Mürren** in 28 minutes.

TIMETABLES

The Swiss Travel System (STS) timetables are essential for traveling on the trains, steamers, cableways, etc. Schedules are posted at all train stations, steamer docks, etc. At the larger stations, the personnel will assist in planning your trip. In most cases, they will provide you with a regional or abbreviated timetable. Ask for it.

> The **Bernese Oberland Region Timetable** is an excellent 24-page directory. Don't be without it. The directory contains a wealth of useful information which will make planning your trips each day much easier. It is available at most train stations and hotels in the area. The Timetable is printed in German with an Explanation of Symbols in English.

If you are interested in the official timetable books (3 Volumes) for the entire **Swiss Travel System**, public and private, they can be purchased at the railway stations and bookstores in Switzerland. This three-volume set weighs close to two pounds.

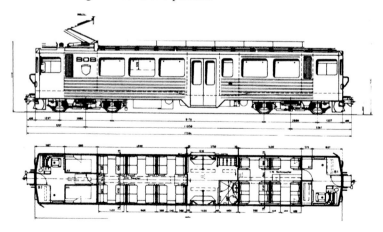

GENERAL INFORMATION

Accommodations	Holidays
Books - Bernese Oberland	Maps
Books - Swiss Cooking	SNTO
Business Hours	Telephone
Festivals & Plays	Temperature
Families - Children	Tipping/Sales Tax
Families - Disabled	What to Wear

ACCOMMODATIONS

The Swiss are known for the high quality of their accommodations and the service they provide. Contact the Swiss National Tourist Office for a copy of the **Swiss Hotel Association Guide** listing 2,700 hotels and pensions. The guide offers a full listing of hotel rates, seasonal schedules, amenities, addresses, telephone and FAX numbers. It is easy to make hotel reservations through your travel agent, or send a FAX to the hotel. Select the hotel you prefer according to price, amenities and location.

If you plan to visit longer than one week, consider staying at a chalet, flat or furnished apartment. Again, get in touch with the Tourist Office for a list of contacts in the town you plan to stay. There are many Youth Hostels. Contact the Tourist Office for a listing of the Swiss Youth Hostels. There is no upward age limit. However, during peak season, members up to 25 years of age have priority. Reservations are advisable for individuals. If you are on a tight budget, consider staying in one of the mountain villages. Choose a small hotel or guest house.

The Swiss Hotel Association also publishes a list of hotels offering special rates to **Senior Citizens** in the off-season. (A senior is defined as a woman over 62 or a man over 65.)

Hotel reservations are needed year-round in the major cities: Bern, Luzern, Zürich and Geneva. In the resort areas, during the high season of July and August, reservations are required. During May, June, September and October, accommodations are generally available in the towns and mountain villages without a reservation. It is always best to make reservations, though, as most hotels do not require a deposit. If you don't plan to keep the reservation be sure to cancel with the hotel.

Please note that the Swiss National Tourist Office does not make hotel reservations.

90

WHAT TO WEAR

In the Bernese Oberland the dress is casual. Pack the same clothing you would wear for a similar season in the northern hemisphere. Keep your wardrobe simple and your luggage light. For the mountains, you will want to layer your clothing with a waterproof windbreaker and light sweaters that can be peeled off, depending upon the temperature.

A good pair of comfortable walking shoes with a cushioned sole is ideal for the mountains. Wear them with a pair of heavy socks and keep some "moleskin" handy, in case you develop a blister. For some of the longer, more strenuous hikes you should consider a pair of lightweight hiking boots to give your ankles support. If you happen to have packed only street shoes, you can still do some of the high elevation walks. No high heels please.

Take along a hat, sunglasses and suntan lotion. If you plan to go up the Jungfrau, pack a pair of gloves. Take along a "sports pouch" to carry your money, film and small items. One person in the group should have a "day pack" to carry the picnic lunch, an extra sweater, a small folding umbrella, a water bottle (or wine) and a Swiss chocolate bar.

FAMILIES AND CHILDREN

The Bernese Oberland is a wonderful place for children, particularly the mountain villages of Wengen and Mürren which do not have cars. Most of the hikes can be done with children, and many walks can be done with children in strollers. Sports such as tennis, swimming and miniature golf are available in most of the villages. Children will delight in the festivals, carnivals and processions.

If you have the opportunity, by all means bring the children to the Bernese Oberland and let them experience the mountains, the food and culture.

FAMILIES AND THE DISABLED

When making travel arrangements for the disabled, the following information may be useful:

- Contact the SNTO for a Fact Sheet and a special hotel guide for the disabled.
- Ask your airline to provide "Meet and Assist" service upon departure and arrival at both airports.
- On Swiss trains, wheelchair passengers travel in a special section of the passenger cars.

FESTIVALS & PLAYS

William Tell Play
Interlaken
Open Air Theatre
2nd Thursday in July to lst Sunday in September
Reservations and warm clothing recommended
Telephone: (036) 22-27-23

Music Festival
Interlaken
May-September15
Telephone (036) 22-21-21

Festwochen (Festival Weeks)
Interlaken
August 15-August 30
Telephone (036) 23-38-00

HOLIDAYS

New Year's Day - January 1, Good Friday, Easter Monday, Ascension, Whit Monday, Christmas Day - December 25, Boxing Day - December 26, National Day - August l.

Regional and local holidays, such as January 2, May 1 (Labor Day) (Corpus Christi, date varies) among others, are observed in many parts of the country.

TIPPING AND SALES TAX

Tips are automatically included on hotel and restaurant bills, as well as hairdressers and most taxi fares. Although tipping is neither necessary nor expected, it is customary to tip hotel porters. There is no sales tax in Switzerland.

TEMPERATURES

The average monthly high and low temperature and the average monthly rainfall for Interlaken:

Temperature
(°F)

	J	F	M	A	M	J	J	A	S	O	N	D
High	36	43	50	59	67	72	74	72	68	59	47	38
Low	23	27	32	38	43	50	54	52	49	41	34	27
Rainfall (Inches)	3.0	2.5	3.3	3.7	4.4	5.5	5.7	4.9	3.9	3.7	3.0	3.6

The temperature in Switzerland is measured in Celsius. To convert from Celsius to Fahrenheit, multiply by 1.8 then add 32.

TELEPHONE

Police	117	Regional Hospital	26 26 26
Fire	118	Emergency Doctor	23 23 23

Ambulance	144	Information	111
Road Service	140	Weather	162
Road Condition	163	Tourist Info	120
Foreign Exch	160	Time	161

The telephone system in Switzerland is well organized and entirely automatic, extending to the remotest corners of the country. You can call Collect to the U.S. and Canada. Country Code is 001. Note: calls made from hotels sometimes have substantial service charges.

A Swiss PTT telephone card (TAXCARD) is available for 10 SF and 20 SF. This allows you to use special pay telephones without the need to worry about the correct change. The price of the call is deducted from the card automatically. It is very convenient when you need to use the telephone.

The TAXCARD is also an advantage when dialing the local numbers for AT&T or MCI for calls to the United States and Canada. For connection to an operator in the United States, the local Swiss telephone numbers are:

AT&T: 155-0011   MCI: 155-0222

BUSINESS HOURS

Banks and Foreign Currency Exchange
Banks are open Monday to Friday from 8:30 a.m. to 4:30 p.m., closed Saturdays, Sundays and holidays. Exchange of foreign currency is also possible at the **Interlaken West** train station 7:30 a.m. to 12:30 p.m. and 1:30 to 6:00 p.m. every day.

Post Offices
Post offices are open Monday through Friday from 8:30 a.m. to 12 p.m. and from 1:30 to 6:30 p.m. Saturday 7:30 to 11 a.m.

Shops
Most shops are open from 8:00 a.m. to 12:00 p.m. and from 1:30 or 2:00 to 6:30 p.m. Saturday until 4:00 p.m.

BOOKS

For those who wish to pursue in greater depth Switzerland and the Bernese Oberland, we have listed several guidebooks. Also listed are books on hiking and cooking. These books are available in many bookstores in the Bernese Oberland.

Baedeker's Switzerland ISBN 0-13-056044-8	328 p.
Essential Switzerland ISBN 0-316-025014-7	128 p.
Fodor's - Switzerland ISBN 0-679-01970-7	356 p.
Michelin Tourist Guide (Green) ISBN 2-06-015-632-0	226 p.
Off the Beaten Track - Switzerland ISBN 0-06-096380-8	285 p.
Switzerland at its Best ISBN 0-8442-9565-5	266 p.
Visitor's Guide to Switzerland ISBN 1-55650-033-8	256 p.

Bernese Oberland Regional Books

Across the Bernese Oberland ISBN 3-905480-05-0	76 p.
The Bernese Oberland Sir Arnold Lunn ISBN 0-04-914053-1	172 p.
Jungfrau Express ISBN 3-280-002087-7	128 p.
Ticket to the Top ISBN 0-9511403-0-2	64 p.

Hiking Books

Bernese Oberland - 30 Walks ISBN 1-85223-415-6	160 p.
Downhill Walking Switzerland ISBN 0-9619276-5-8	82 p.
Foot-Loose in the Swiss Alps ISBN 0-87156-102-6	44 p.

| Jungfrau Region Hiking Guide | 128 p. |
| ISBN 3-259-03081-6 | |

| Morrow Guide to Backcountry Europe | 336 p. |
| ISBN 0-688-001016-4 | |

| 100 Hikes in the Alps | 224 p. |
| ISBN 0-916890-72-4 | |

| Walking Switzerland | 272 p. |
| ISBN 0-89886-1137-3 | |

| Wandering | 329 p. |
| ISBN 0-7965-22-094 | |

Swiss Cooking

Cooking in Switzerland - Kaltenbach
Culinary Excursions through Switzerland - Widmer
Little Swiss Cookbook - Martinet
Swiss Cooking - Mason
The Swiss Cookery Book - Guggenbuhl

MAPS

The Swiss Topographic Bureau in Wabern (suburb of Bern) issues maps, such as the selection below. All maps are 1:25000 and available at bookstores or sport shops in Switzerland.

Grindelwald	#1229
Lauterbrunnen (Wengen)	#1228
Mürren	#1248
Gemmi	#1267
Adelboden (Kandersteg)	#1247
Brienz	#1209
Beatenberg	#1208
Niesen	#1227

Lauterbrunnen-Jungfrau Region Wanderkarte (1:33333)
This map describes 44 hikes and climbs from an easy 40-minute walk to a very strenuous 4-hour climb to the Schmadrihütte at 7,440 feet.

Grindelwald Wanderkarte (1:25000)
A detailed map of the trails surrounding Grindelwald.

Kandersteg Wanderkarte (1:25000)
Identifies the easy walks and strenuous climbs in the area.

Thuner-und Brienzersee Wanderkarte (1:50000)
Identifies lakes, villages, transportation, trails as far south as Mürren.

SWISS NATIONAL TOURIST OFFICES (SNTO)
IN NORTH AMERICA AND THE UNITED KINGDOM

The Swiss National Tourist Offices in the United States, Canada and the United Kingdom are an excellent resource to use in planning your trip. Contact them early for maps, brochures and information regarding the locations you plan to visit. Request information for hotels and any special interest or activity you may wish to pursue.

New York	608 Fifth Avenue New York, NY 10020 Telephone: (212) 757-5944 FAX: (212) 262-6116
Chicago	150 N. Michigan Avenue Chicago, IL 60601 Telephone: (312) 630-5840 FAX: (312) 630-5848
Los Angeles	222 N. Sepulveda Boulevard El Segundo, CA 90245 Telephone: (310) 335-5980 FAX: (310) 335-5982
San Francisco	260 Stockton Street San Francisco, CA 94108 Telephone: (415) 362-2260 FAX: (415) 391-1508
Toronto	154 University Avenue, Suite 610 Toronto, Ontario M5H 3Y9 Telephone: (416) 971-9734 FAX: (416) 971-6425
London	SNTO, SWISS CENTRE 1 New Coventry Street London W1V 8EE Telephone: 71/734 1921 FAX: 71/437 4577

AFTERWORD

We have written **Swiss - Bernese Oberland** to share with you some of the personal experiences we have enjoyed over the years exploring this region. We have enjoyed many times the Trips and the Excursions, the food and the wine described in this book.

Wengen has always been our headquarters. We love this sunny village and the people. We like to ride the mountain trains, the funiculars, the cable cars, the steamers and walk the trails. While the BIG trips we have done many times - the Jungfrau and the Schilthorn - below are the trips we enjoy every year to get renewed and close to nature.

MÄNNLICHEN TO KLEINE SCHEIDEGG - Trip #6
> 1½ hour downhill walk towards the Jungfrau Massif.
> Picnic along the way or lunch at Kleine Scheidegg.

STEAMER TRIP - Trip #4
> A trip on one of the steamers from Interlaken to Thun
> or to Brienz. Explore the old town, then take the train
> back to Interlaken.

GRÜTSCHALP TO MÜRREN - Trip #2
> 1½ hour walk through the forest and pasture with the
> mountains always changing before you. Lunch in Mürren
> or picnic along the way.

BACHALPSEE - Trip #3
> A spectacular mountain lake. Take the gondola to First,
> then an easy walk to the lake. Lunch at First or picnic
> along the way.

OESCHINENSEE - Trip #7
> Don't miss a trip to Kandersteg and the Oeschinensee.
> This is not a tour bus stop. The Oeschinensee is one of
> the most beautiful clear mountain lakes.

In this book we have shown the minimum times for completing each trip. For those who want to get an early morning start and see as much as possible, two trips can be accomplished most days. However, the half day trips, such as the Jungfrau, Schilthorn, Oeschinensee, etc. can easily take all-day depending on when you start and how much time you spend enjoying the sights, lunch, etc.

Enjoy the trips and the area to the fullest. Let us know if we have missed anything or how this book can be improved. We look forward to hearing from you. Our address is: **c/o Intercon Publishing, P.O. Box 18500, Irvine, CA 92713, USA.**

PHOTOGRAPHS

PRINTING

This book was printed by Digital Quickcolor, Inc., Irvine, California on a Heidelberg GTO-DI press using Direct Presstek Imaging Technology. This process transfers computer data directly to the press eliminating the use of film and metal plates.

INDEX

NOTES

NOTES

ORDER FORM

Please send me **Swiss-Bernese Oberland**
by Philip & Loretta Alspach

International

_____**Swiss-Bernese Oberland** @ **$16.95**   _____

1st Book Air Mail @ $5.00   _____

1st Book Surface Mail @ $3.00   _____
(3-4 weeks)

Each Additional Book add $2.00   _____
(to same address)

Total U.S. Funds enclosed $_____

Domestic

_____**Swiss-Bernese Oberland** @ **$16.95**   _____

1st Book Air Mail @ $2.50   _____

Each Additional Book add $1.00   _____
(to same address)

Calif. Residents add 7.75% Tax @ $1.30   _____

Total U.S. Funds enclosed $_____

Payment enclosed   ☐ Check   ☐ Money Order

Ship to:

Name _____

Address _____

_____

City/State _____

Country _____

Send Order to: **Intercon Publishing**
P.O. Box 18500
Irvine, CA 92713
U.S.A.

TEL: (714) 955-2344   FAX: (714) 833-3156